Bohemond I, Prince of Antioch

TEMPLAR KNIGHTS

Bohemond I,
Prince of Antioch
A Norman Soldier of Fortune and
Crusader 1050-1111

Ralph Bailey Yewdale

LEONAUR

Bohemond I, Prince of Antioch
A Norman Soldier of Fortune and
Crusader 1050-1111
by Ralph Bailey Yewdale

First published under the title
Bohemond I, Prince of Antioch

Leonaur is an imprint
of Oakpast Ltd

Copyright in this form © 2010 Oakpast Ltd

ISBN:978-0-85706-210-9 (hardcover)
ISBN: 978-0-85706-209-3 (softcover)

http://www.leonaur.com

Publisher's Notes

In the interests of authenticity, the spellings, grammar and place names
used have been retained from the original editions.

The opinions of the authors represent a view of events in which he
was a participant related from his own perspective,
as such the text is relevant as an historical document.

The views expressed in this book are not necessarily
those of the publisher.

Contents

SOLDIERS OF THE FIRST CRUSADE

Preface

Ralph Bailey Yewdale entered the University of Wisconsin in 1910. In his junior year he was President of Philomathia and was elected to the Student Conference and to the Iron Cross (Honorary Senior Society). The following year he was elected to Phi Beta Kappa and received the degree of Bachelor of Arts. After one year of graduate work at Wisconsin and receiving a Master of Arts' degree, he was appointed to a Procter fellowship at Princeton.

At Princeton Yewdale was a brilliant student and constantly at work on some problem. He had many interests, especially in literature and music, which made him a delightful companion. He was popular with his instructors and associates in the Graduate College, and won their admiration by his ability. He received the Ph.D. degree in 1917.

He entered the army as private in Company B, 330th Machine Gun Battalion, 85th Division, September, 1917. He was made Sergeant in the same organization, February, 1918, and was commissioned Lieutenant of Infantry, May, 1918. In May and June, 1918, he was stationed at Camp Lee, Virginia, then transferred to Company L, 69th Infantry, General Wood's Division, at Camp Funston, Kansas, in June, 1918. On September 7, 1918, he was ordered to the Historical Branch, General Staff, U.S.A., and in December, 1918, sent to Paris with the Peace Commission, where he remained until July, 1919. He retired from the service in August, 1919, and was appointed Assistant Professor of History at the University of Wisconsin, 1919- 1921. He died November 25, 1921 (aged 29 years).

Yewdale had assembled the material for this thesis for his degree at Princeton, and had written the first draft, but had actually revised only a few pages in the type-written form. This is unfortunate, because his meticulous revision would have added many a felicitous touch. This thesis, however, is such a useful addition to our knowledge that it ought to be published, even in a form that would have seemed to Yewdale far from satisfactory. The editor's task has been confined to making the corrections in the manuscript which were inevitable. Love for a former student and companion, respect for his scholarship, would not permit any attempt to add aught to his work.

At Wisconsin Yewdale taught modern history. He became interested in Talleyrand's career, and in his researches found important new material which he was preparing to incorporate in an article. He had already prepared a note on "An Unidentified Article by Talleyrand, 1796," which was published in the *American Historical Review*, October, 1922. The article, unfortunately, is not near enough completion to be published.

His teachers and associates would wish that I attempt some statement of our feeling of loss to the cause of learning. It is futile. We believed in him; we admired him; we loved him.

CHAPTER 1

Bohemond's Early Life

The history of Norman expansion in the Mediterranean world in the eleventh century is little more than the story of the personal fortunes of the house of Hauteville. It is doubtful whether there can found in the history of medieval Europe a more remarkable family than that which, within less than three-quarters of a century, with little more at its disposal than its own sheer native genius for conquest and government, succeeded in subduing to its power not only all of southern Italy and Sicily, but Cilicia and northern Syria as well, and which menaced, for a time, the very existence of the Byzantine Empire, at that period the greatest military power in Christendom. Like the conquerors of England, these other Normans established a Norman state in a foreign and hostile land, and if William of Normandy bulks larger in history than Robert Guiscard, the discerning historian will realize that the successes of the former were more imposing in the same degree as his resources were greater. William invaded England as the greatest feudal lord in France; Robert came into Italy with no other material possessions than his horse and armour.

One may catch in the pages of the contemporary historians of southern Italy and Greece, in Geoffrey Malaterra, in William of Apulia, and in Anna Comnena, the Byzantine princess who knew these adventurers only to hate and fear them as the most dangerous enemies of her father's empire, something of the character of these Normans, de Hautevilles and others,—stout-limbed and ignorant of fear; crafty, vengeful, and shrewd, with an astuteness which might sink to the level of mere roguish cunning or rise to the masterly finesse of a Byzantine diplomat; "crueler than the Greeks and fiercer than the Saracens";[1]

---

1 Arnulfus, *Gesta archiepiscoporum Mediolanensium*, in MGSS, 8, p. 10.

grasping and avaricious beyond all bounds, yet willing to give with an open hand when policy demanded; greedy for power and impatient of restraint, gifted to a remarkable degree with a genius for imitation; eloquent, with a realization of the value of flattery; fickle and inconstant in their dealings with strangers, yet possessed of an indomitable persistence and a willingness to endure toil, hunger, and cold, if anything was to be gained.[2]

Southern Italy, though seemingly destined by nature to form a single state with the Abruzzi and the sea as its boundaries, had not yet gained, on the eve of the Norman conquest, the unity which the genius of the Normans was alone to give it. The Byzantine Greeks after the reconquest of their ancient possessions by the generals of Basil the Macedonian and Leo the Wise, whose names, quaintly and incorrectly transliterated, stare out from the Latin pages of Muratori, still ruled over Apulia, the heel of the peninsula, and most of Calabria, while their claims of sovereignty extended, in typical Byzantine fashion, far beyond the actual limits of the dominion of the *basileus*. Along the western sea-board, lay the three maritime states of Gaëta, Naples, and Amalfi, thriving on the profitable trade with the Levant, and now owning, now repudiating the authority of Constantinople.

Shouldering these merchant states on the east and marching with the Byzantine themes along their northern boundaries lay the three Lombard states of Capua, Benevento, and Salerno, all of them independent and ceaselessly striving with the Greeks and with each other for the hegemony of southern Italy. On the other side of the Straits of Messina, as through all the rest of Sicily ruled the Arabs, the warlike Aglabites of Kairouan, whose oft-repeated raids had, throughout two centuries, terrified and laid waste the maritime districts of southern Italy.

The warring ambitions of emperor, *basileus*, and pope, the wrangling and jangling of the Lombard princes,[3] the severity and unpopularity of the Greek rule, and the domestic difficulties of the Byzan-

2 Gaufredus Malaterra, *Historia Sicula*, in Muratori, RISS, 5, p. 550, contains the classic description of Norman character; for Norman avarice see Guillermus Apuliensis, *Gesta Roberti Wiscardi*, in MGSS, 9, pp. 242, 245, 254, 260; for Norman love of power, see Aimé, *L'ystoire de li Normant*, edited by O. Delarc (Rouen, 1892), p. 10; see also Anna Comnena, *Alexias*, edited by L. Schopen and A. Reifferscheid (Bonn, 1839-1878), 2, pp. 127, 222.

3 Guil. Ap., p. 244.
Illis principibus dominandi magna libido
Bella ministrabat.

tine Empire on the eve of the Normans' arrival, all served to make southern Italy ripe for conquest. The meeting of the Lombard rebel, Melus, with a group of Norman pilgrims at Monte Gargano in 1015 or 1016, and his request that on their return home they seek to enlist mercenaries for service in the Lombard cause against the Greeks was an event of untold importance for the history of southern Italy and of the Byzantine Empire as well. With the coming shortly afterwards of the first Norman adventurers who had answered the call of the returned pilgrims or the solicitations of the Lombard agents who may have accompanied them, begins the first stage in the Norman conquest of southern Italy. It was not until some twenty years later that the first of the de Hautevilles arrived in Italy.

Tancred de Hauteville, the head of the house, lived at Hauteville-la-Guichard, near Coutances in Normandy, where he held a fief. He was married twice; by his first wife, Muriella, he had five sons; by the second, Fressenda, seven sons, the eldest of whom was Robert, nicknamed Guiscard, or the Wily,[4] the ablest by far of the twelve sons and destined to be the father of Bohemond, and the youngest Roger, the future conqueror and count of Sicily. Tancred's narrow lands could not long contain nor serve to satisfy the ambitions of his numerous and adventurous progeny, and eight of the sons chose to seek their fortunes in the south of Italy.

Like the other Normans who had preceded them thither, the sons of Tancred began their Italian careers as mercenaries, selling their swords indiscriminately to Greek and Lombard. The power of the Norman mercenaries increased with their numbers, and it was not long before they began to speak as masters, when once they had spoken as servants. "*Nouz non intrames en la terre pour issirent si légement; et molt nouz seront loing à retorner là dont nouz venîmes,*" said the blunt-spoken Normans to Michael Duceianus, the Byzantine *catapan*.[5] Ten years after the arrival of Robert Guiscard in 1045 or 1046, the conquest of the land by the Normans under the leadership of the de Hautevilles is well under way. With the events of this audacious enterprise, we are not here concerned.[6]

---

4 Guil. Ap., p. 256.
Cognomen Guiscardus erat, quia calliditatis
Non Cicero tantae fuit aut versutus Ulixes.
5 Aimé, p. 71.
6 The Norman conquest of southern Italy and Sicily has been dealt with in the following works: Ferdinand Chalandon, *Histoire de la domination normande en Italie et en Sicile* (Paris, 1907), 1, the latest and best book on the subject; (continued next page.)

Anna Comnena, whose pages are filled, naturally enough, with much talk of the Normans, has given us a vivid sketch of the appearance and personality of Guiscard, in which she has pictured him as a great, handsome barbarian, with yellow hair, long beard, ruddy complexion, dull blue eyes, and a tremendous voice; on the whole pleasing and seemly in appearance, with a touch of imperial dignity in his presence. "He was, as I remember hearing from many, a handsome man from the top of his head to his feet." A typical Norman, he is intolerant of restraint, brave and skilful as a soldier, greedy and avaricious to the last degree, and extremely crafty and cunning.[7] The young Norman *condottiere*, who was destined one day, as the vassal and ally of the pope, to assume the proud title of "duke of Apulia and Calabria, by the grace of God and St. Peter, and with their aid future duke of Sicily," and who was to betroth one of his daughters to the son and heir of a Byzantine emperor, spent his early years in Italy as a brigand and a highway robber in the mountains of Calabria.[8] It is during this initial stage of his Italian career that his first marriage took place, a union which was to result in the birth of a single son, Marc Bohemond, the future prince of Antioch, and the subject of this essay.

On coming to Apulia to visit his brother, Drogo, Robert, Aimé tells us, was met by a certain Girard of Buonalbergo, a Norman lord with holdings north of Benevento, who not only offered him an alliance with the promise of two hundred horsemen to aid him in the conquest of Calabria, but also suggested that he marry his aunt, Alberada, a proposal which Robert regarded favourably; and after the objections of Drogo, who rejoiced in the title of count of Apulia and the position of head of the house of Hauteville in Italy, had been overcome, the marriage took place.[9] We cannot fix the date at all exactly. Aimé regarded the marriage as the beginning of Robert's good fortune and of his rise in the world;[10] we may, therefore, assume that it took place before the great victory at Civitate in 1053 raised high the prestige of Guiscard, and may fix it in the early 1050's. The Norman bride,[11]

O. Delarc, *Les Normands en Italie depuis les premières invasions jusqu'à l'avènement de S. Grégoire VII* (Paris, 1883); Lothar von Heinemann, *Geschichte der Normannen in Unteritalien* (Leipzig, 1894); Jules Gay, *L'Italie méridionale et l'empire byzantin* (Paris, 1904).
7 Anna, 1, pp. 49-51, 293-294. Cf. Guil. Ap., pp. 256, 259-260.
8 Aimé, pp. 108-110; Malaterra, pp. 553-554; Anna, 1, p. 51.
9 Aimé, pp. 110-111. For the marriage, see also Malaterra, p. 557. Cf. Anna, pp. 51 ff.
10 Aimé, p. in: "*Ceste choze fu lo commencement de accrestre de tout bien à Robert Viscart.*"
11 The name is probably of Norman origin, and, in addition, Malaterra asserts that she was of Robert's own race; Malaterra, p. 557. (Continued next page.)

in spite of the fact that she was the aunt of the lord of Buonalbergo, must have been extremely young at the time of her marriage, for she was still alive in 1122. [12]

The only issue of this marriage was the son, who was baptized Marc, [13] but who rendered famous, and gave as a family name to a long line of Latin princes in the East, the nickname of Bohemond. The exact date of his birth is not known, but it may be placed between 1050, the earliest probable date of his father's marriage to Alberada, and 1058, [14] the date of Guiscard's second marriage. The nickname Bohemond, according to Ordericus Vitalis, the Norman historian, was given to him by his father, who had recently heard at a banquet a droll tale about a certain "Buamundus Gigas," and who evidently considered the name appropriate for his own giant son. [15] The nickname lasted, and finally supplanted the baptismal name altogether. [16]

I have discovered nowhere that the name was borne by anyone else before Bohemond, son of Guiscard, made it celebrated throughout Europe. It later became a fairly common name. See the indices of the *Monumenta*, Bouquet, and the *Acta Sanctorum*.

Nicknames or descriptive epithets were, of course, very common in the Middle Ages—witness Robert Guiscard, William Iron-Arm, Pandolf Iron-Head, Robert Curthose, Roger Borsa, etc.

We know nothing of Guiscard's married life with Alberada, except that in 1058 or earlier he divorced her on the grounds of consanguinity,—so frequently an excuse in the early Middle Ages,

---

The fact that her husband afterwards divorced her on the grounds of consanguinity proves that she was, at least in part, of Norman extraction. Cf. Robertus Monachus, *Historia Hierosolymitana, in Rec., Hist, occ.* 3, p. 855: "*Sed a matre quae Apuliensis exstitit, retinuit vestigia.*"

12 See *infra*, this chapter.

13 Malaterra, p. 557; Ordericus Vitalis, *Historiae ecclesiasticae libri tredecim*, edited by Auguste le Prévost (Paris, 1838-1855), p. 212; Erasmus Gattola, *Ad historiam abbatiae Cassinensis accessiones* (Venice, 1734), 1, pp. 205-206.

14 Malaterra, p. 558.

15 Ord., 4, p. 212. I have been unable to discover anything about this legendary giant, Bohemond. Förstemann's attempt to derive the name, Bohemond, from a combination of the name of the German tribe of the Boii with the suffix, *mund*, guard, is only a conjecture. Ernst Förstemann, *Altdeutsches Namenbuch* (Bonn, 1900), 1, cols. 324-325, 1133. I am also unable to explain why Anna Comnena refers to Bohemond as Βϊαμοῦντον τὸν Σανίσκος .Anna, 1, pp. 233, 208, *et passim*.

16 See the grant of August, 1090, in Gattola, *Accessiones*, 1, pp. 205- 206, in which Bohemond styles himself "*Marcus, qui et Abboamonte Rubberti Duels filius*." This is the only document I have found in which Bohemond employed his baptismal name.

when a veering passion or policy made a divorce desirable—and married Sigelgaita, sister of Gisulf, the Lombard prince of Salerno.[17] He seems to have made ample provision for the support of Alberada and her infant son.[18]

A number of documents enable us to discover something of Alberada's later life. She was married twice after her divorce from Robert, first to Roger of *Pomareda* or *Pomaria*, and after his death to Richard the Seneschal, son of Drogo, and hence nephew of Robert, by whom she seems to have had a son named Robert.[19] In a donation of 1118 to the Church of the Holy Trinity of Venosa for the souls of her relatives, she refers to "Robert Guiscard, the unconquered duke . . . and *his* son, Bohemond."[20] The same expression is employed in her donation to the Church of St. Mary in the Valley of Jehosaphat, and in the same document she refers to Robert and Bohemond as her *consanguinei*, which may appear odd, until it is remembered that Robert was really *consanguineus* with her, and had divorced her for that very reason.[21]

In her documents, Alberada signs herself as "Lady of Colobraro and Policoro," possessions situated in Basilicata near Angelona. She was certainly alive as late as July, 1122, for in that month she made a grant to the monastery of La Cava,[22] but died before September 1125, probably leaving her possessions to her grandson, Bohemond II, for in that month we find him granting the bridge of Policoro to the Church of the Blessed Martyr Anastasius of Carbono;[23] by September of the next year, Alexander and Richard of Chiaromonte, nephews of

---

17 Aimé, pp. 168-170; Malaterra, p. 577; Guil. Ap., p. 262.
18 *Chronica monasterii Casinensis auctoribus Leone Marsicano et Petro Diacono*, in MGSS, 7, p. 707. The medieval French translator of Aimé evidently misunderstood the meaning of his Latin original in this connection, and has made it appear that Robert made provision for Sigelgaita and her infant son, instead of for Alberada and her son, after his second marriage. Leo who used the original Latin version has reproduced the correct sense of the passage. Aimé, p. 170.
19 Guiseppe Crudo, *La SS. Trinità di Venosa* (Trani, 1899), pp. 207-208.
20 Crudo, pp. 207-208.
21 C. A. Garufi, "*I documenti inediti dell' epoca Normanna in Sicilia*" (Palermo, 1809), in the *Archivio storico siciliano, Documenti, 1 ser.*, 18, p. 70. This document exists only in the form of later confirmations. The original grant was anterior to 1113, for in that year Pascal II confirmed the donation. See Henri-Frangois Delaborde, *Charles de Terre Sainte, provenant de l'abbaye de Notre-Dame de Josaphat* (Paris, 1880), p. 25.
22 Heinrich Wilhelm Schulz, *Denkmaeler der Kunst des Mittelalters in Unteritalien* (Dresden, 1860), 4, p. 1.
23 Ferdinando Ughelli, *Italia sacra* (Venice, 1717-1722), 7, pp. 75-76.

Alberada, [24] have received the town of Policoro as a grant from the young Bohemond. [25] Alberada was buried in the Church of the Holy Trinity at Venosa near the tomb of Guiscard and his brothers, and an inscription of later date above her tomb recalls her connection with the illustrious house of Hauteville, and the burial place of her crusader son at Canosa.

Guiscardi coniux Aberada hac conditur arca
Si genitum quaeres hunc Canusinus habet. [26]

Almost nothing is known about Bohemond's early years. He probably learned to read and write Latin, [27] and reared as he was in the polyglot civilization of southern Italy he must have been in a position to acquire a knowledge of Greek and Arabic, but it is extremely doubtful whether he took advantage of the opportunity. [28] He left his mother for his father, when we do not know, and was undoubtedly brought up together with Roger Borsa and Robert's other sons by Sigelgaita. The years of his youth and early manhood must have been spent in his father's army, for during the great revolt of Guiscard's Norman vassals in 1079, we find him commanding a detachment of Guiscard's troops at Troia, where he sustained a serious defeat at the hands of his cousin, Abelard, [29] and, in 1081, when Guiscard undertook the invasion of the Byzantine Empire, Bohemond was already so experienced a soldier that he was chosen to act as his father's second-in-command.

---

24 Crudo, p. 207.
25 Ughelli, 7, p. 77.
26 Emile Bertaux, *L'art dans l'Italie méridionals* (Paris, 1904), 1, pp. 320–321.
27 Bohemond subscribes a grant to the Genoese of July 14, 1098, with the formula, "*Signum mei Boamundi, qui. hanc chartam donationis fieri iussi, firmavi et testes firmare rogavi*," the use of the first person being evidence, according to Hagenmeyer, that the subscription was written by Bohemond himself. *Die Kreuzzugsbriefe aus den Jahren 1088-1100*, edited by Heinrich Hagenmeyer (Innsbruck, 1901), pp. 156, 310. (Cited as HEp.)
28 According to Bartolfus de Nangeio, *Gesta Francorum Iherusalem expugnantium, Rec. Hist, occ.*, 3, p. 499, Bohemond was able to converse with Firuz, the man who betrayed Antioch, in the latter's language, which, in his negotiations with the Crusaders, was Greek, but Anna's statement that her father sent an interpreter with the commission which opened peace negotiations with Bohemond in 1108, makes it probable that he knew little or no Greek. Anna, 2, p. 217. That he was not acquainted with Arabic before he went to Syria is proved by the statement of the *Gesta Francorum* concerning his action at the siege of Marra, "*Boamundus igitur per interpretem fecit loqui Sarracenis majoribus. . . .*" *Anonymi Gesta Francorum et aliorum Hierosolymitanorum*, edited by Heinrich Hagenmeyer (Heidelberg, 1890), p. 407. (Cited as HG.)
29 *Chronicon breve Nortmannicum*, in Muratori, RISS, 5, p. 278 (6).

CHAPTER 2

The Wars With the
Byzantine Empire, 1081-1085

In 1080, the ambitious Guiscard turned toward new fields of conquest. The sharp spurs of the Abruzzi, the principality of the equally warlike Normans of Capua, and the interdiction of the pope precluded all thought of further expansion in Italy; his brother Roger had almost completed the conquest of Sicily; he therefore turned his attention to the east, toward the Byzantine Empire, whose troops he had so often routed in his Italian campaigns. [1]

The Eastern Empire had fallen upon evil days. A succession of weak and incapable rulers had made possible the rise of a powerful landed aristocracy in Asia Minor, which, deriving its power from the enormous rentals of its estates, and from the exploitation of the offices of the civil service, could disregard at will the legislation of an impotent imperial government, whose policies were directed less from the council-chamber than from the cloister or the gynaecium. The civil wars, which so vexed the middle years of the eleventh century, had at the same time increased the importance, and impaired the efficiency of the imperial armies, which withstood with ever-growing difficulty the persistent attack of the Petcheneg in the north, and of the Seljukian Turk in the east.

The year 1071 saw at once the capture by the Normans of Bari,

---

1. The Norman had small respect for the Greek, either as a warrior or as a man. Aimé, pp. 17-18: "*Qui bien cerchera li auter et 1'ystoire especialement de Troya, trovera que li Grex ont plus sovent vainchut per malice et par traison que par vaillantize*"; *Ibid.*, p. 25: "*Et commencerent a combatre contre li Grez, et virent qu'il estoient comme fames*"; Guil. Ap., pp. 242, 246; Malaterra, p. 579: "*. . . gens deliciis et voluptatibus, potiusquam belli studiis ex more dedita.*"

16

the last Greek stronghold in Italy, and the almost total annihilation of an imperial army at Manzikert, at the hands of Alp Arslan. Within a decade, the greater part of Asia Minor was lost to the Turks. [2]

In this chaos the old Byzantine army practically disappeared. The regiments which fell at Manzikert might in time have been replaced had the Asiatic themes remained in the hands of the empire. But within ten years after the fall of Romanus IV those provinces had become desolate wastes: the great recruiting-ground of the imperial army had been destroyed, and the damage done was irreparable.... It is no longer the old Byzantine army which we find serving under Alexius Comnenus and his successors, but a mass of barbarian adventurers, such as the army of Justinian had been five hundred years before.[3]

So low had sunk the Byzantine prestige that the court of the same Empire, which under Nicephorus Phocas had haughtily rejected the proposal of Otto the Great for a matrimonial alliance, now saw its offer of a similar plan summarily dismissed by the *parvenu* duke of Apulia and Calabria.[4]

Guiscard had little difficulty in discovering a pretext for his attack on the Empire. After having rejected Michael VII's proposals of a marriage between the former's brother and one of his daughters, Guiscard lated agreed to a plan for the marriage of one of his daughters to Michael's son, Constantine, and the young woman was duly sent to Constantinople, where she entered the gynaecium, preparatory to her marriage.[5] In 1078, Nicephorus Botaniates usurped the Greek throne, sending Michael to a monastery and Guiscard's daughter to a convent.[6] This slight to his ducal dignity was for Guiscard a sufficient cause for war, but it was not until 1080 that domestic affairs allowed him to take advantage of the opportunity, and to begin his preparations for the campaign.[7]

---

2. For a description of the Empire in the eleventh century, see Carl Neumann, *Die Weltstellung des byzantinischen Reiches vor den Kreuzzügen* (Heidelberg, 1894).

3. Charles Oman, *A History of the Art of War: The Middle Ages from the Fourth to the Fourteenth Century* (London, 1898), p. 221. Cf. Hans Delbrück, *Geschichte der Kriegskunst im Rahmen der politischen Geschichte* (Berlin, 1900-1907), 3, pp. 206-207.

4. For Michael VII's first two matrimonial proposals, see Ferdinand Chalandon, *Essai sur le règne d'Alexis 1ᵉʳ Comnène* (Paris, 1000), pp. 61-62.

5. Anna, 1, pp. 49-57; Aimé, pp. 297-298; Malaterra, p. 579; Guil. Ap., p. 275.

6. Anna, 1, p. 58; Malaterra, p. 579; Guil. Ap. p. 279.

7. For the whole war, 1081-1085, see the monograph of Karl Schwarz, *Die Feldzüge Robert Guiscards gegen das byzantinische Reich* (Fulda, 1854) and Chalandon, *Alexis*, ch. 3.

In this same year, desirous of justifying the course he was pursuing and of arousing the enthusiasm of his subjects for the invasion of the Empire, he produced a Greek who claimed to be the ex-*basileus*, Michael, escaped from his Greek monastery prison to seek Guiscard's aid against the usurper. The contemporary writers disagree as to the origin of this person, who was maintained in imperial splendour by Guiscard for a considerable period of time, but a majority of the best sources realize that the man was an impostor.[8] There can be no doubt now that the whole episode was a daring hoax planned by Guiscard himself for the deception of his own and of Nicephorus' subjects; even the upright Gregory VII lent himself, perhaps innocently, to the solemn farce.[9]

The campaign, which had already been graced by the benediction of Guiscard's spiritual and temporal overlord, was inaugurated in March, 1081,[10] by sending to the coast of Albania an armed force under Bohemond, recently appointed as second-in-command to his father, with instructions to occupy and lay waste the region about Avlona, and probably with further orders to attack Corfu. The occupation of the town and gulf of Avlona, which provided an excellent base for the main expedition, was successfully accomplished, and, in addition, Canina and Hiericho were taken. Bohemond then moved south and captured Butrinto on the mainland opposite Corfu, after which he began a campaign against the island itself.[11]

Guiscard sailed from Otranto in May, after appointing Roger, his oldest son by Sigelgaita, as regent of his Italian possessions, and designating him as his successor.[12] The sources vary widely in their estimates of the size of Guiscard's army, from Ordericus Vitalis' ten thousand to Anna Comnena's thirty thousand men in

---

8. Anna, 1 pp. 58-62; Malaterra, p. 579; Guil. Ap., pp. 282-283; *Anonymi Barensis Chronicon*, in Muratori, RISS, 5 p. 153; *Anonymi Vaticani Historia Sicula, Ibid.*, 8, col. 768; Lupus Protospatarius, *Chronicon*, in MGSS, 5, p. 60.

9 Gregorii VII *epistolae et diplomata*, in Migne, *Pat. Lat.*, 148, cols. 580-581.

10. An. *Bar. Chron.*, p. 153.

11. Anna, 1, p. 70; Guil. Ap., pp. 282-283; Malaterra, p. 582; Lupus, p. 60.

12 Anna, 1, pp. 181, 232; cf. *Ibid.*, 1, pp. 75-76; Guil. Ap., p. 283; Ord., 3, p. 171. Cf. Chalandon, *Domination normande*, 1, pp. 267-268: "*Il laissa à son fils Roger, qu'il désigna comme son successeur éventuel, l'administration de ses États, sauf la Calabre et la Sicile, dont il confia le gouvernement au comte Roger.*" It is evident from the following passage from William of Apulia, which he cites as his authority, that Chalandon has misread his source.

Ius proprium Latii totius et Appula quaeque
Cum Calabris Siculis loca dux dat habenda Rogero.

18

150 ships. [13] The Norman historians naturally tend to minimize the size of Guiscard's army and to exalt the number of Greek troops who opposed them. Schwartz has estimated that Guiscard had fifteen thousand men under his command, but the candid investigator must admit that the data at his disposal do not allow him to make an estimate which would be even approximately correct. [14] Malaterra, basing his remark upon the accounts of men who participated in the expedition, asserts that there were not more than thirteen hundred horsemen in the army, and according to the rather doubtful testimony of Romuald of Salerno, Robert had only seven hundred knights at Durazzo. [15]

The expedition was composed not only of Normans but of Lombards, Italians, and doubtless some Greeks of southern Italy as well. [16] If we may believe the prejudiced Anna, whose remarks are in part confirmed by Malaterra, the war was not a popular one, and Guiscard had to resort to the sternest and most pitiless measures to swell the number of his forces. [17] The Normans of southern Italy had lost much of the seafaring skill of their forefathers, [18] and a large part of the fleet was composed of ships from Ragusa and other cities of the Dalmatian coast, [19] although Guiscard had built some ships of his own. [20]

Before Guiscard had completed his preparations for the invasion of the Empire, the ambassador whom he had dispatched to Constantinople for the purpose of demanding reparation from Nicephorus returned with the news that Nicephorus had been deposed by a new revolution, and that Alexius Comnenus, former grand domestic of the Empire, was now *basileus*. [21] With the overthrow of Nicephorus disappeared Guiscard's chief reason for taking up arms, but he was not to be cheated of his opportunity and undertook against the brave and active Alexius the war which he had planned against the sluggish and unwarlike Nicephorus.

Fortunately for the Byzantine Empire, the revolution had brought to the throne an able soldier and artful diplomat. Like the best and most successful of the Byzantine *basileis*, Alexius Comnenus is distin-

---

13. Anna, 1, pp. 74-75; *Chron. mon. Cas.*, p. 738; Ord. 3 p. 170; Malaterra, p. 583.
14. Schwartz, p. 9.
15. Malaterra, p. 582; Romualdus Salernitanus, *Chronicon*, in MGSS, 19, p. 410.
16. Guil. Ap., p. 286.
17. Anna, 1, pp. 68-69; Malaterra, p. 583.
18. Guil. Ap., p. 268; "*Gens Normannorum, navalis nescia belli. . . .*"
19. *Ibid.*, pp. 282, 285; Heinemann, 1, p. 313.
20. Malaterra, p. 580.
21. Anna, 1, pp. 71-73.

guished by the indomitable perseverance and the fertility of design, which aided him in beating off the attacks of the enemies of his empire. It is sufficient glory for this life-long enemy of the Normans to have defeated the two most illustrious conquerors of the house of Hauteville. [22]

Guiscard, crossing the Adriatic, touched at Avlona and other ports on the Albanian coast, [23] and after joining Bohemond, undertook the conquest of Corfu, which he completed with no great difficulty, [24] while another portion of the fleet operating farther to the south, captured Bundicia on the Gulf of Arta. [25] The army then started north for Durazzo, its main objective, part on the fleet with Guiscard, the remainder travelling with Bohemond over the land route.[26] The latter portion of the Norman forces captured Levani on the Semeni River as it moved on Durazzo, [27] but the fleet, less fortunate, encountered a terrific storm while rounding Cape Glossa and many of the vessels were lost. [28] Guiscard, however, with courage and confidence undiminished, on June 17 began the siege by land and sea of Durazzo, the western terminus of the ancient Via Egnatia, and the most important Greek city on the Adriatic. [29]

Alexius, in the meanwhile, had not been idle, and had entered into negotiations with Abelard and Hermann, the disgruntled nephews of Guiscard, with the emperor Henry IV, and with Venice, with a view to a joint attack upon the Normans, while at the same time he had replaced the untrustworthy governor of Durazzo, Monomachus, with George Palaeologus. [30]

The results of Alexius' negotiations with the great maritime republic of the Adriatic were soon apparent, when a Venetian fleet appeared before Durazzo in July or August.[31]

22. Chalandon, *Alexis* is an excellent biography of the *basileus*, somewhat prejudiced, however, in his favour.

23. Andreas Dandulus, *Chronicon*, in Muratori, RISS, 12, p. 248; *Chronici Amalphitani Fragmenta*, in Muratori, *Antiquitates*, 1, p. 368; Malaterra, p. 582.

24 .Guil. Ap., p. 283; Malaterra, p. 582; Lupus, p. 60. *An. Bar. Chron.*, p. 153 supplies the date: "*decimo die stanti Magi.*"

25. Guil. Ap., p. 283.

26. Anna, 1, p. 183.

27. An. *Vat. hist. Sic.*, col. 769.

28. Anna, 1, pp. 183-184; Guil. Ap., pp. 283-284.

29. Anna, 1, p. 187.

30. Anna, 1, pp. 172-177.

31. The date may be deduced from the fact that the annals of Lupus Protospatarius and the *Anonymous Chronicle of Bari*, both of which (continued next page.)

The sources differ somewhat in their description of subsequent events. According to Malaterra, the Venetian fleet was hotly attacked by the Norman vessels and so badly beaten by sunset, that it was forced to promise to surrender on the next day. The Venetians, however, spent the night in refitting their vessels, and in erecting on their masts fighting-tops from which missiles could easily be launched at the enemy ships, so that on the next day when the Venetians came out, ready for battle instead of surrender, the unprepared Norman fleet was compelled to gaze helplessly on, while the fleet of the Republic sailed past it into the harbour of Durazzo, breaking the blockade and reopening communications with the beleaguered city. The Venetians were occupied that night and the day following with further preparations, but on the night of the third day they sailed out again and gave battle to the Norman fleet. One of the Norman vessels, the *Cat*, was destroyed by Greek fire, but the Normans had the satisfaction of disposing of a Venetian ship of similar value, and after a rather indecisive struggle, both fleets drew off, the Venetians to Durazzo, the Normans to their position off the shore. [32]

According to Anna Comnena, Guiscard, on the arrival of the Venetians, sent out the Norman fleet under Bohemond to force them to acclaim the pseudo-Michael and himself, which the Venetians promised they would do on the morrow, but entering the port of Durazzo, they spent the night in building their fighting-tops, and when on the next day, after they had put out from the port, they were summoned by Bohemond to salute the pseudo-Michael and Robert, they answered his demand with jeers and insults. Bohemond, not brooking such treatment, gave the order to attack, and in the battle which followed, had his own ship sunk, and was forced to board another of his vessels. The Venetians, after routing the Norman fleet, landed on the shore and attacked Guiscard's camp, while at the same time a Greek force under George Palaeologus made a sortie from the city. After a successful engagement, the Venetians returned to their ships and the Greek garrison to the city. [33]

Guiscard had pushed the siege of Durazzo energetically, but Pal-

begin the year with September I, place the battle with the Venetian fleet at the end of their accounts of the year 1081. Lupus, p. 60; *An. Bar. Chron.*, p. 153.

32. Malaterra, pp. 583-584.

33. Anna, 1, pp. 193-194. William of Apulia, who otherwise follows in this portion of his narrative the same tradition as Anna, agrees with Malaterra that the engagement extended over a period of three days. Guil. Ap., p. 275.

aeologus was a skilful soldier, and the machines which Guiscard had built were burned by the garrison of the town. On October 15, Alexius, with a hastily-collected army, in which almost a dozen nationalities were represented, camped near Durazzo. Against the advice of Palaeologus, who had come by sea from Durazzo to attend the war-council, and some others of his officers, who suggested a blockade and starvation campaign against the Normans, Alexius decided to risk a battle with Guiscard. [34] On October 17, when it became evident that Alexius was preparing for battle, Guiscard burned his ships, that his men might fight with greater desperation. [35]

The Norman army was drawn up for battle early on the morning of October 18, with Guiscard holding the centre, the Norman count, Amicus, the wing which rested upon the sea, and Bohemond, who had been in charge of the army while his father snatched a few hours' sleep after midnight, the other wing. [36] Alexius had conceived an ingenious plan of battle, but the rashness of the Varangian Guard, the desperate charges of the Norman cavalry, who rallied at the exhortations of Sigelgaita, and the treachery of a portion of Alexius' troops, spelled disaster for the Greeks, and the end of the day saw the slaughter of the valiant English guard, the rout of the imperial army, and the sack of Alexius' camp. [37] The *basileus*, who had fled to Ochrida, and thence to Salonika, experienced for some time the greatest difficulty in raising an army, and Guiscard was left unmolested to continue his siege of Durazzo. [38]

The duke established winter quarters on the Deabolis not far from Durazzo, and had the satisfaction of receiving the surrender of the minor fortresses throughout the Illyrian province. [39] In January or February, 1082, Durazzo itself now lacking the presence of Palaeologus, who had been cut off from the city during the battle of October 17, was betrayed to Guiscard by a Venetian named Dominic, who had been corrupted by the promise of a marriage with Guiscard's beautiful niece, the daughter of William of the Principate. [40]

---

34. Anna, 1, pp. 200-204.
35. Malaterra, p. 584; Anna, 1, p. 207; Guil. Ap., p. 286.
36. Anna, 1, p. 208; Malaterra, p. 584.
37. Anna, 1, pp. 217-221; Malaterra, p. 584; Guil. Ap., pp. 286-287; Lupus, p. 61; *An. Bar. Chron.*, p. 154; Dandulus, p. 249. See Oman, pp. 164-165.
38. Anna, 1, pp. 221, 225 ff.
39. Malaterra, p. 584; Guil. Ap., p. 288.
40. Malaterra, pp. 584-585; Guil. Ap., pp. 288-289. *The Anonymous Chronicle of Bari* fixes the surrender on February 21, while Lupus thinks (continued next page.)

Guiscard, with the whole Albanian littoral now in his possession, next undertook in the spring, the invasion of the interior. The Albanian hinterland presents extraordinary difficulties to an invader from the west, the almost unbroken mountain chains, which run in a north-south direction, and the lakes of the interior forming so many natural defences. Three avenues into the interior lie open to the invader, the Shkumbi, the Viosa, and the Vyros valleys. Up the Shkumbi valley ran, and still runs, the old Roman Via Egnatia, which, winding around the heads of the Ochrida, Prespa, and Ostrovo lakes, continues on its way to Salonika.[41] A hostile native population can do enormous damage to an invading army, but there is reason to believe that the Illyrians, Slavs, and Bulgars of these regions were by no means favourably inclined to the fortunes of the *basileus*, for the Normans met with little resistance from the natives.

Guiscard seems to have moved inland without encountering effectual opposition anywhere; fortress after fortress surrendered to him, and, according to Malaterra, even the important post of Castoria with its garrison of three hundred Varangians, fell to him without a blow. "Fear of him," to use the rather extravagant words of the Norman historian, "made the whole Empire tremble, even as far as the Royal City."[42] His march into the heart of Greece was checked not by the force of Greek arms but by the more insidious powers of Byzantine diplomacy, always one of the Empire's most effective weapons; for a messenger arrived from southern Italy in April or May, 1082, with the news that his dominions were aflame with revolt and that the emperor, Henry IV, had marched on Rome, while a letter from the pope begged him to return post-haste. Handing over the command of the expedition to Bohemond, Guiscard hastily left for Italy.[43]

Anna Comnena becomes virtually our only detailed source for subsequent events. Her sense of chronology is notoriously weak, her knowledge of geography almost equally so. As a result, it is extremely difficult to construct a credible account of the campaign from this

it took place in January. *An. Bar. Chron.*, p. 154. Lupus, p. 61. Anna says that the city was surrendered by the Venetians and Amalfians who had wearied of the siege. Anna, 1, p. 223. Lupus also refers to the "*traditionem quorundem Veneticorum.*"
41. Lyde, Lionel W., and Lieut.-Col. A. F. Mockler-Ferryman, *A Military Geography of the Balkan Peninsula* (London, 1905); Gottlieb Lucas Friedrich Tafel, *Via militaris Roinanorum Egnatia* (Tübingen, 1842).
42. Malaterra, p. 585. Anna, 1, p. 244, seems to place the capture of Castoria in the period after Guiscard's departure for Italy.
43. Anna, 1, p. 232; Malaterra, p. 586; *Gregorii VII epistolae,* cols. 619-620.

point on, for Anna in her account has Bohemond marching and countermarching over the Balkans in the most bewildering fashion, as the following narrative and the use of a good map will disclose.

Bohemond, now left to face a general little older in years, but far more experienced than he in the direction of large bodies of troops, was, with the exception of one egregious blunder, to acquit himself well in the year and a half of fighting which followed Guiscard's departure. If we may accept the word of Anna Comnena, the Norman plan of campaign now underwent a decided change, for instead of moving eastward from Castoria and marching on Salonika, Bohemond turned to the southwest for the purpose of occupying and subduing more effectually the territory between Castoria and the Adriatic coast, for, in spite of the many fortresses which had capitulated to Guiscard's arms, a considerable number were still held by their Greek garrisons.

The sources give no explanation for the changes in the Norman plan of campaign, but it may be conjectured that Guiscard, not anticipating that affairs in Italy would detain him long from returning to the theatre of war, ordered Bohemond to devote his time, during his own absence, to consolidating the Norman position, without running the risk of seeking a decisive pitched battle with Alexius. But the situation in Italy was far more serious than Guiscard probably realized, and it was not until 1084 that he was free to return to Albania.

Bohemond, aided by the presence of a considerable body of Greek troops, who, despairing of the fortunes of Alexius, had deserted to his ranks, now marched into Epirus, captured Janina, far to the south and west of Castoria and almost directly east of Butrinto. [44] He rebuilt the citadel of the town, added a new tower to the walls, and devastated the villages and fields of the surrounding country.

Alexius, who was at Constantinople, learned of Bohemond's activities in May, and completing his military preparations, marched on Janina. An ingenious plan to break the Norman line by sending against it light chariots bristling with spears, was anticipated by Bohemond, who, probably informed in advance of the movement, opened his line at the critical moment, allowed the chariots to pass through, and then fell upon and routed the Greek army. [45] Alexius fled to Ochrida, where he undertook the reorganization of his army, and, after ob-

44. Chalandon, *Alexis*, pp. 85-86, conjectures that Bohemond, relying upon the friendship of the Vlachs living about Janina, captured the city in order to have a base of operations in the south similar to Durazzo in the north.
45 Anna, 1, pp. 236-238.

taining reinforcements from the Vardar valley, again marched against Bohemond, who had moved south and was now besieging Arta. The *basileus*, probably hoping to counterbalance in some degree the paucity of his numbers or the unwarlike spirit of his troops, again resorted to stratagem, and on the night before the battle had his men scatter three-cornered pieces of iron about a portion of the battle-field, in the hope that the Norman cavalry in charging his centre would cripple its horses so badly that it could easily be shot down by the Greek infantry, while, at the same time, a spirited attack on both of the wings would complete the destruction of the Norman army.

Bohemond, however, learned in advance of the plan, and, on the morrow, his centre, instead of advancing over the ground so skilfully prepared by the Greeks, remained stationary, while both wings engaged and routed the extremities of the Greek line, and eventually compelled the *basileus* and the centre to flee, as well. The victory was complete; the Byzantine army was hopelessly shattered; and Alexius was compelled to return to Constantinople, to undertake again the task of raising fresh troops.[46]

Anna, at this point in her narrative, describes the capture by the Normans of a number of fortresses in the north and east. Peter of Aulps takes the two Polobus, and the count of Pontoise occupies Uskub, while Bohemond himself captures Ochrida, onetime capital of the great Bulgarian empire. Unable to take the citadel of the city, he advances along the Via Egnatia to Ostrovo, which he attacks unsuccessfully; thence he marches by way of Soscus, Verria, Servia, and Vodena, attacking many fortresses, often without result. From Vodena he goes to Moglena, where he rebuilds the ruined citadel, and leaving a garrison under the command of a Count Saracen, he makes his way to Asprae Ecclesiae on the Vardar River, where he remains three months. While sojourning here, he discovers that three of the commanders, the count of Pontoise, Reginald, and William, who had probably been tampered with by Alexius, are planning to desert.

Ralph of Pontoise makes good his escape to the *basileus*, but the other two are apprehended, and after undergoing trial by battle, William is blinded by Bohemond, and Reginald is sent back to Italy where Guiscard metes out to him the same punishment. Bohemond next marches west to Castoria, which Anna thinks is still in the hands of the Greeks, and then advances south into Thessaly to the important

---

46. Anna, 1, pp. 239-242; Malaterra, p. 588. Guil. Ap., pp. 290-291, makes one battle out of the two and places it at Janina.

town of Larissa, where he plans to winter.

Without doubt, some of the fortresses enumerated in the fore-going passage were captured by Guiscard before his departure for Greece, or by Bohemond before his march into Epirus. Indeed, one may be permitted to doubt whether Bohemond ever retraced his steps north again after invading Epirus, a move which both Chalandon and Schultz, relying upon Anna, have unquestionably accepted.

It is at this stage that Anna chronicles the capture by the Normans of Pelagonia, Trikala, and Castoria, although Castoria had probably been captured before Guiscard's departure. If Bohemond had really intended to winter at Larissa, he must have changed his plans, and probably contenting himself with leaving a besieging party there, he seems to have gone to Trikala, where he very probably wintered, and whence he sent out an expedition which captured Tzibiscus.

In the spring of 1083, he returned to Larissa, which he reached on April 23. The city had for six months withstood the Norman siege, the Greek commander, in the meanwhile sending letters to Alexius, giving him news of the siege, and in all probability asking for aid.

The *basileus* appeared in Thessaly in due time, his army augmented by a force of seven thousand Turks, and gave battle to the Norman army. This time, the stratagem which Alexius had conceived did not reach Bohemond's ears. Deceived by the sight of the imperial stand-ards which Alexius had handed over to Melissenus and Curticius, and thinking that they had before them the main body of the imperial army, the Normans under Bohemond and the count of Brienne en-ergetically engaged the Greek forces, which fell back according to a preconcerted plan. When he perceived that the Normans were a considerable distance from their camp, Alexius led his men from the ambush where they had hidden the night before, and attacked and occupied with little difficulty the Norman camp, while the slingers, whom he had dispatched after the count of Brienne's pursuing cavalry, played havoc with the Norman horses.

Bohemond seems to have withdrawn from the battle after the first charge, for the messengers whom the count of Brienne sent to him with the news, found him on a little island in the Salabrias River, eat-ing grapes and jesting over Alexius' defeat. On learning of the change in his fortunes, he hastily collected a company of Norman knights, and rode to the top of a hill overlooking Larissa, where a Greek charge on his position, made against the advice of the *basileus*, was bloodily repulsed. Another detachment of Greek and Turkish troops, which had been sent to anticipate a possible Norman attempt to cross the Salabrias, was routed and driven down to the river. Alexius' victory was not complete, but Bohemond had lost his camp and baggage, the siege of Larissa had been raised, and the imperial army still held the field.[47]

On the next day, Bohemond with the remains of his army crossed the river and marched to a wooded pass between two mountains, where he pitched his camp. On the day following, a body of Turkish and Sarmatian slingers, who had been sent to harass the Norman forces, ventured too far into the pass and were attacked and routed by Bohemond's troops.[48]

Bohemond now decided upon a retreat, for the defeat before Larissa, and the loss of his camp and supplies forced him to give up his Thessalian campaign. He moved west to Trikala, where he found a body of his troops who had fled thither after the first battle at Larissa, and thence north to Castoria. By this retreat, Thessaly passed once more into Alexius' hands.[49]

It is during this period, or possibly somewhat earlier, that peace negotiations of some sort took place between Alexius and Bohemond, a fact upon which the chronicles are silent. A *typikon* of the Convent of the Virgin of Petritzus at Philippopolis, dated December, 1083, contains the signature of Euthymius, patriarch of Jerusalem, who had been at Salonika at the request of the *basileus*, "for the purpose of making peace with the accursed Frank (ἕνεκεν εἰρήνης τοῦ ἀλάστορος Φράγκου)."[50] There can be no doubt that the reference is to Bohemond, but, unfortunately, we know nothing more about the negotiations.

Alexius now resumed his secret negotiations with Bohemond's officers. He urged them through messengers to demand from Bohemond their pay, which was now long in arrears, and if Bohemond was unable to obtain the money, to force him to return to Italy; for their services they were to receive valuable gifts and employment in the Greek army or a safe-conduct home, providing they did not wish to enter the imperial service.

A sufficient number in the Norman army were found to carry out Alexius' wishes, and Bohemond, unable to obtain money for the troops, was forced to leave for Italy. Handing over Castoria to the

---

47. Anna, 1, pp. 242-253; Guil. Ap., pp. 291-292.
48. Anna, 1, pp. 253-255; Guil. Ap., p. 292.
49. Anna, 1, p. 255.
50. P. Bezobrazoff, *Materiali dlya istorii vizantiiskoi imperil*, in *Zhurnal ministerstva narodnavo prostvyeshtshyenyiya*, November, 1887, 254, pp. 76-77.

count of Brienne and the two Polobus to Peter of Aulps, he went to Avlona.[51]

The news that Castoria had fallen to the Greeks in October or November, and that virtually all of his officers and troops, with the exception of the count of Brienne, had deserted to Alexius, reached him while he was tarrying in the Albanian seaport.[52] A Venetian fleet had recaptured the city of Durazzo in the summer of 1083, with the exception of the citadel, which was still held by its Norman garrison,[53] and this, with Avlona and Corfu, was probably the only strong position in Norman hands at the end of 1083. It is impossible to fix definitely the time of Bohemond's departure for Italy; the fact that he does not seem to have met his father at Salerno until the latter's completion of the campaign against Henry IV in the spring of 1084, may lead one to the assumption that Bohemond wintered at Avlona.[54]

The defeat at Larissa had been the decisive point in the war, but the causes of the Norman failure lay deeper. The savage mountains of the Balkans, the difficulty of obtaining supplies, the constant depletion of the army, due not only to battle and disease, but to the necessity of garrisoning the captured fortresses, and, no doubt, to desertion, the impossibility of securing reinforcements to use against the Emperor of the East, while Guiscard stood in need of them in his struggle with the Emperor of the West, all militated against the success of the Normans.

Guiscard, downcast at the news of the complete failure of his son's campaign, nevertheless undertook preparations for a new campaign against Alexius, and since his vassals were now completely subdued, he left Italy in October, 1084, with a fleet of 120 vessels, and accompanied or preceded by his four sons, Bohemond, Roger, Robert, and Guy.[55] Roger and Guy, who had been sent ahead to occupy Avlona, which had probably been recaptured by the Greeks after Bohemond's departure, fulfilled their mission, and were met by their father on the coast between Avlona and Butrinto.[56]

Guiscard was anxious to sail south to raise the siege of his garrison

51 Anna, 1, p. 256; Guil. Ap., p. 292.
52 Anna, 1, pp. 269-272, 280.
53 Guil. Ap., p. 292; Anna, 1, p. 195. See Schwartz, p. 40.
54 Anna, 1, pp. 280-281.
55. Anna, 1, p. 282; Guil. Ap., pp. 293-294; *An. Bar. Chron.*, p. 154. According to Anna, Guy had been secretly won over by Alexius. I am convinced that this is a misplaced reference to Guy's treason during the expedition of 1107. See *infra.*, p. 120.
56. Anna, 1, p. 282.

28

at Corfu, but violent storms compelled him to lie over at Hiericho for two months. [57] Able at length to put to sea, on arriving at Corfu and entering the port of Cassiope, he was attacked and defeated by a Venetian fleet, which had come to Corfu at the request of Alexius and established headquarters in the harbour of Passarum.

Three days later, Guiscard was again defeated by the Venetians. [58] Taking advantage of the absence of most of the swift Venetian ships which had been sent home with the news of the victories over the Normans, Guiscard and his four sons, each commanding five large fighting-vessels and a number of smaller craft besides, attacked and overwhelmingly defeated the fleet of the Republic. According to Lupus Protospatarius, more than a thousand men perished in the battle, five ships were captured, and two sunk with their crews. [59]

Guiscard, having raised the siege of his beleaguered garrison on Corfu and regained control of the island, sailed southwards and went into winter-quarters on the mainland, on the banks of the Glycys River, where he beached his ships. [60] During the winter, the plague broke out in the Norman army, carrying off many officers and men, and Bohemond, who had contracted the disease, received permission from his father to return to Italy for medical treatment. [61] In the spring of 1085, Guiscard again resumed his campaign, and directed Roger against the island of Cephalonia. He had planned to follow his son, but was taken ill and died at Cassiope on Corfu on July 17. in the presence of Roger and Sigelgaita. [62] The usual dark suspicions of treachery and poison in connection with his death are to be found in the later chronicles. [63]

Roger, Guiscard's eldest son by Sigelgaita, had, as we have already seen, been designated by the duke as his successor, before the departure

---

57. *Ibid.*, pp. 195-196; Guil. Ap., p. 293.

58. Anna, 1, pp. 283-284.

59. Anna, 1, pp. 284-285; Guil. Ap., pp. 293-294; Dandulus, cols. 249- 251; Lupus, p.61; *An. Bar. Chron.*, p. 154; Romuald Sal., p. 411. Romuald places the defeat of the Venetians in November, 1084; the *Chronicle of Bari*, in January, 1085.

60. Anna, 1, p. 196; Guil. Ap., pp. 294-295. According to William, Guiscard later left the Glycys, and went north to Bundicia, where he wintered.

61. Anna, 1, p. 196; Guil. Ap., p. 295.

62. Guil. Ap., pp. 296-297; *Necrologium Casinense*, in Muratori, RISS, 5, col. 75; *Chron. brev. Nort.*, p. 278 (6); *An. Bar. Chron.*, p. 154; Anna, 1, pp. 288-289; Dandulus, col. 252. See Schwartz, p. 45.

63. Ord., 3, pp. 181-187; Willelmus Malmesbiriensis, *De gestis regum Anglorum libri quinque*, edited by William Stubbs (London, 1887-1889), 2, pp. 321-322; *Gesta regis Henrici secundi Benedict: abbatis*, edited by William Stubbs (London, 1867), 2, p. 201.

of the expedition in 1081,[64] a decision which must be ascribed almost wholly to the personal influence of Sigelgaita, for Roger was inferior in almost every quality, mental and physical, to the son of Alberada. A twelfth century chronicler tells us that Guiscard had planned, in case he were successful in his campaigns in the East, to make Bohemond emperor of the Byzantine Empire, and himself ruler of a great Mohammedan empire beyond—a fantastic enough story.[65] Whether it is true or not, Guiscard had failed, and no arrangement seems to have been made for Bohemond's future.

Roger took advantage of his half-brother's absence in Italy to hasten to Bundicia and have himself recognized by his father's forces there; he then returned to Cephalonia to inform the Norman troops of his father's death. Soon after his departure from Bundicia, the Norman army there, terrified by the realization of what the death of their leader meant, broke into a wild stampede for the shore, and boarding their vessels as best they might, set out for Italy, while Roger, removing the garrison from Cephalonia, sailed for Otranto with his mother and the body of his father.[66] Such was the melancholy and inglorious conclusion of the wars of Robert Guiscard with the Eastern Empire.

---

64. Roger had been recognized as Guiscard's successor by the duke's vassals as early as the spring of 1073. Aimé, p. 289.
65. Richardus Pictaviensis, *Chronica*, in MGSS, 26, p. 79.
66. Guil. Ap., pp. 297-298.

CHAPTER 3
Bohemond in Italy, 1085-1095

Roger's first act on returning to Italy was to bury his father in the Church of the Holy Trinity at Venosa. [1] Relying on the aid of his uncle, Roger, count of Sicily, the son of Guiscard next undertook to secure the recognition of his father's vassals, and was acclaimed duke in September, 1085, in spite of the opposition of the disinherited Bohemond. [2] For his support, Count Roger received in full ownership the Calabrian castles which he had formerly held in joint tenure with Guiscard. [3]

Roger, nicknamed Borsa by his father, because of his habit of counting and recounting the coins in his purse, [4] was destined to prove himself scarcely worthy, in the long reign which was to follow, of the title which he bore and of the lineage he boasted. Well-meaning for the most part, he lacked his father's strength and energy; although capable at times of acts of fiendish cruelty, he did not possess the more martial virtues which were indispensable in repressing the turbulent Norman nobles. As a result, he frequently found it necessary to call upon his uncle, Roger of Sicily, for aid which was dearly bought with valuable concessions of territory in southern Italy. [5] He was not wanting in at least the more manifest forms of personal piety, as one may judge from his numerous gifts and foundations in the interest of the Church; it is said that the grateful monks of La Cava still pray for his soul. [6]

---

1. Guil. Ap., p. 298; Anna, 1, p. 289; Malaterra, p. 589.

2. *Ibid.*; Lupus, p. 62. See Chalandon, *Domination normande*, 1, p. 287.

3. Malaterra, p. 589; Chalandon, *Domination normande*, 1, p. 288.

4. Wil. Malm., 2, pp. 452-453.

5. Guil. Ap., p. 289; Malaterra, p. 591. The latter gives a flattering characterization of Roger, but even he admits that Roger was lenient to a fault. Cf. Romuald. Sal., pp. 414-415.

6. Paul Guillaume, *Essai historique sur l'abbaye de Cazva d'après des documents inédits* (Naples, 1877), p. 53.

Taking advantage of the departure of Count Roger for Sicily, Bohemond began a rebellion against his brother. Malaterra thinks it was brought about by Bohemond's ambition, while Fra Corrado speaks of Roger's ill-treatment of Bohemond. [7] Whether or not Bohemond had possessions of his own from which he could draw troops it is impossible to say. [8] If we may trust Ordericus Vitalis, Bohemond fled from Salerno to Capua on the return of Roger and Sigelgaita to Italy, and received aid against his brother from Prince Jordan and other friends.[9] The campaign was a complete success for Bohemond; Oria surrendered to him, and aided by the adventurers who flocked to his standards in the hope of booty, he ravaged the lands about Taranto and Otranto.

Roger was forced to make peace and to cede to Bohemond the important cities of Oria, Taranto, Otranto, and Gallipoli, and the lands of his cousin, Geoffrey of Conversano, possessions which included Conversano, Montepiloso, Polignano. Monopoli, Brindisi, Lecce, Nardo, Castellana, Casaboli, and Sisignano. [10] These lands he undoubtedly held as a vassal to Roger. Bohemond, no longer a landless noble, had become in a very short time one of the most powerful lords in southern Italy, in spite of the efforts of his half-brother. How different the new duke of Apulia from his predecessor!

Peace was made before March, 1086, for in that month we find Roger, Bohemond, and Robert Guiscard the Younger all signatory to a grant of Sigelgaita to Orso, archbishop of Bari. [11] The signatures of Roger and Bohemond are also affixed to a grant by Roger to Orso, dated May, 1086, [12] and to a donation of the port of Vietri to the Abbey of La Cava, also dated May, and issued at Salerno. [13] A grant to the Monastery of the Holy Trinity at Venosa, made in the same month,

---

7. Malaterra, p. 591; *Epistola fratris Conradi Dominicani prioris sanctae Catherinae in civitate Panormitana,* in Muratori, RISS, 1, pt. 2, p. 277.

8. According to Romuald, Guiscard left Bohemond nothing. Romuald. Sal., p. 412.

9. Ord., 3, pp. 182-183, 307-308.

10. Malaterra, p. 591; Dom. Morea, *Chartularium del monastero di s. Benedetto di Conversano* (Monte Cassino, 1892), p. 37.

11. *Codice diplomatico Barese* (Bari, 1897-1914), 1, pp. 56-58.

12. *Ibid.,* pp. 58-59.

13. Guillaume, pp. 12I-13. Di Meo gives the digest of a document signed by Roger and Bohemond, issued at Salerno and attested by the same notary and witnesses as the preceding document, but dated May, 1087. In all probability, di Meo was guilty of an error in copying the date of the document, and wrote 1087 for 1086. Alessandro di Meo, *Annali critico-diplomatici del regno di Napoli della mezzana eta* (Naples, 1795-1819), 8, p. 289.

also bears the signatures of Roger and Bohemond. [14] An undated grant by Bohemond to the same monastery of the possessions in Giovenazzo of a certain Basil of Trani may be placed tentatively in this year. [15]

An extensive confirmation of earlier donations to the Abbey of La Cava, made by Roger in May, 1087, carries the subscription of Bohemond, [16] as does a grant in favour of Orso, archbishop of Bari, dated June. [17]

In September or October, 1087, Bohemond began a second war against Roger, and launching a surprise attack on his brother's troops at Fargnito, north of Benevento, was defeated. The engagement must have been little more than a skirmish, for although a large number of Bohemond's men were taken prisoners, there was only one man killed in the whole action. [18] Bohemond probably then returned to Taranto, for we find him issuing in October the confirmation of a grant to the Monastery of St. Peter in Taranto. [19]

At some time before or during the war, he had induced Mihera, lord of Catanzaro, one of Roger's rebellious Calabrian vassals, who had seized upon the city of Maida, to renounce his brother's suzerainty and become his own vassal. The winning over of Mihera was a profitable move for Bohemond, for it gave him a foothold in Calabria; as a result, in the ensuing campaign, all the fighting seems to have taken place in Calabria, and Bohemond's Apulian possessions were never menaced.

Bohemond began the Calabrian campaign by marching on Cosenza, which surrendered on his promise to destroy the hated citadel which Roger had garrisoned with his troops; he was admitted into the city, and began an attack upon the fortress. Word of the revolt was carried to Roger in Apulia, who immediately sent for his uncle, Roger of Sicily, but before either of them could arrive at Cosenza,

---

14. Giuseppe del Giudice, *Codice diplomatico del regno di Carlo I e II d'Angio* (Naples, 1863-1902), 1, p. 25; Crudo, p. 175; Chalandon, *Domination normande*, 1, p. 289, n. 5.
15. Crudo, p. 175.
16. Lothar von Heinemann, *Normannische Hersogs-und Königsurkunde aus Unteritalien, Programm* (Tübingen, 1899), pp. 5-11.
17. *Cod. dip. Bar.*, 1, pp. 59-61.
18. Romuald. Sal., pp. 411, 412. The date is supplied by Lupus Protospatarius, p. 62; "*mense Septembri factus est grandis terremotus per totam Apuliam . . .; tunc enim coepta est guerra inter Rogerium ducem et Boamundum, fratrem eius.*"
19 Francesco Trinchera, *Syllabus Graecarum membranarum* (Naples, 1865), pp. 65-66. The document is interesting from the fact that it is in Greek. It has the following subscription: "*σιγίλλιον γενόμενον παρ' ἐμοῦ Βοαμούνδου υἱοῦ τοῦ πανυπερλάμπρου δουχὸς.*"

Bohemond had captured and destroyed the citadel. The duke, effect-
ing a meeting with his uncle, attacked and burned Rossano which had
also risen in revolt, and then marched on Maida, where he expected
to find Bohemond, but the lord of Taranto, on hearing of his brother's
approach, had left Hugh of Chiaromonte [20] in command at Cosenza
and had gone to Rocca Falluca, evidently fearing that he would be
besieged at Cosenza. On learning of their error, the two Rogers set
out for Rocca Falluca, but encamping at a place which Malaterra
designates as *Lucus Calupnii*, they sent messengers to Bohemond and
Mihera with overtures of peace and the suggestion that a meeting take
place at Sant' Eufemia. Mihera appeared at the appointed time, but
Bohemond returned to Taranto without meeting his brother, so that
the war dragged on for almost two years.

Sometime in the first half of 1089, a peace was arranged between
the two brothers, by the terms of which Roger ceded Maida and
Cosenza to Bohemund. The latter, however, had promised the citizens of Cosenza that he would not erect a fortress in their city, and
since Roger had made a similar promise to the citizens of Bari, it
appeared to be to the advantage of each of the brothers to effect an
exchange, so that Bari was handed over to Bohemond, and Roger
took back Cosenza. [21] This exchange took place towards the end of
August, 1089. [22]

Bohemond had undoubtedly gained by the exchange. Bari was the
richest and most important city in Apulia; its trade with the Orient
was extensive and profitable, and its position was such that it practically guaranteed to its possessor the control of the Apulian littoral. [23] The
gain of Bari and of possessions in Calabria now assured to Bohemond
almost as much power as Duke Roger himself possessed. [24]

Modern historians have, almost without exception, dignified Bohemond with the title of prince of Tarentum or Taranto, in spite of
the fact that there is no evidence either in the documents or the

---

20. This person was probably a relative of Alberada by marriage.
21. Malaterra, pp. 592-593.
22. Joannes archdiaconus Barensis, *Historia inventionis II s. Sabini episcopi Canusini*, in
AASS, 9 Feb., 2, pp. 330-331; *An. Bar. Chron.*, p. 154. See di Meo, 8, pp. 302-303.
23. W. Heyd, *Histoire du commerce du Levant au moyen-âge* (Leipzig, 1885-1886), 1, p.
97; Gay, p. 584.
24. Radulphus Cadomensis, *Gesta Tancredi in expeditione Hierosolymitana, in Rec., Hist,
occ.*, 3, p. 606: *Ejus imperio quicquid est oppidorum et urbium, a Siponto ad Oriolium in
maritima, omnes prorsur in montanis et campestribus locis, omnes fere serviebant: ad haec sua
tam urbes quam oppida Appuli montes Calabrique plurima sustinebant."

contemporary historians of the existence of this title during his lifetime. In his documents, before the assumption of the title of prince of Antioch, he almost invariably signs himself as "*Boamundus, filius Roberti ducis*"; his officers refer to him as "*dominus Boamundus*," or dignify him with the more fulsome title of "*dominus meus excellentissimus ac gloriosus Boamundus inspiratus a Deo*," [25] an expression which smacks of the style of a Byzantine chancery. The only document I have found dated prior to his departure on the First Crusade in which he uses the title, prince, is a thirteenth century copy of a grant of October, 1093, in which he refers to himself as "*Ego Boamundus dei gratia princeps Roberti ducis f. . . .*" [26] It is quite evident that the copyist has introduced into the document a title which was not found in the original. The title, prince of Taranto, came into existence probably during the first half of the twelfth century; Bohemond II does not seem to have used it in his documents, but a confirmation of Roger II's dated 1154 refers to Bohemond I as prince of Taranto and Antioch. [27]

In spite of the fact that the city of Taranto later gave its name to the lands which Bohemond now held, it is to be noted that Bari and not Taranto was the most important city in his dominions. Bari had been the centre of the Greek administration in Italy and the residence of the imperial *catapan* from the end of the tenth century on, and it retained much of its importance as a governmental centre under the Normans, for Guiscard and his successors with the typical adaptability of the Normans took over a large part of the Byzantine administration. Bohemond's chief local agents keep the title of *catapan*, and the Greek term, *critis*, still serves as the denomination of a judicial official of the Norman administration. [28] Not only were the Greek offices retained but Greeks were sometimes chosen to fill them, witness the mention of a "*Nikifori sue barine curie protonotarii*" in a document issued by one of Bohemond's *catapans*. [29] Even Bohemond's seal is pure Byzantine in type; the obverse bears a bust of St. Peter, holding a cross over his right shoulder, and executed in typical Byzantine style, with the legend "ΟΠΕ ΤΡΟ" the reverse has the usual Byzantine formula "ΚΕΒΟΗΘΗΤΩΣΩ ΔΥΛΟΝΒΟΥ ΜΟΥΝΤΗ." [30]

25. *Cod. dip. Bar.*, 5, pp. 37-38, et passim.

26. *Ibid.*, 1, pp. 65-67.

27. *Cod. dip. Bar.*, 2, p. 222.

28. *Ibid.*, 5, 36-37, 37-38, 38-40, 55-57, *et passim*.

29. *Cod. dip. Bar.*, pp. 37-38.

30. Arthur Engel, *Recherches sur la numismatique et sigillographie des Normands de Sicile et d'Italie* (Paris, 1882), pl. 2, 1; (Continued next page.)

The Hellenizing activities of the Greek *basileis* throughout a number of centuries had resulted in the creation in southern Italy of a considerable Greek influence, especially noticeable in the heel of the peninsula and in Calabria, an influence which was perpetuated by the close relation which existed between the Norman nobles and the Greek *basileis*, [31] and by the trade of Bari, Brindisi, and Taranto with the Byzantine East.

It is somewhat more difficult to determine the degree of contact between Apulia and the Mohammedan lands of the Mediterranean, the proximity of Sicily and the fact that Count Roger on several occasions introduced Saracen forces into southern Italy [32] must have made Bohemond familiar in some degree with the Mohammedan civilization of .that island, while the extensive commerce of the Apulian coast cities with the Mohammedans of Syria and Palestine, [33] and the pilgrimages of Apulians to the Holy Land brought them into close contact with countries, destined within a few years to become the seat of Bohemond's conquests. [34] Bohemond, furthermore, had already encountered the Turks, in the shape of the Seljukian mercenaries in Alexius' army. [35]

In the summer of 1089, Urban II, who had been elected pope in March, 1088, [36] came into southern Italy, and on August 1 was at Capua. [37] Bohemond, hearing of his arrival, dispatched messengers to him, inviting him to come to Bari. [38] On September 10-15, Urban held a council at Melfi, which was attended by Duke Roger, and a large number of the nobles of Apulia and Calabria, [39] including Bo-

---

Nicolao Putignani, *Vindiciae, vitae et gestorum s. thaumaturgi Nicolai archiepiscopi Myrensis*, etc. (Naples 1753-1757), 2, p. 312, n. b.; *Cod. dip. Bar.*, 5. Suggeli, Tav. 1, No. 4.

31. Constantinople was a convenient refuge for the fugitive vassals of the Norman dukes.

32. Malaterra, pp. 596, 597.

33. Heyd, 1, p. 97.

34. Orso, archbishop of Bari, made a pilgrimage to Jerusalem in 1088. Joannes Barensis, p. 330. It is interesting to note that the merchants of Bari, who in 1087 brought back with them the bones of St. Nicholas from Myra in Asia Minor, had obtained them while on their way to the port of the city of Antioch with a fleet of grain-ships. Ord., 3, p. 206 and n. 2.

35. Guil. Ap., pp. 285-286.

36. *Chron. mon. Cos.*, p. 761.

37. Philip Jarré—S. Loewenfeld, *Regesta pontificum Romanorum* (Leipzig, 1885), 5406.

38. *Cod. dip. Bar.*, 1, pp. 64-65.

39. Joannes Dominicus Mansi, Sacrorum *conciliorum nova et amplissima collectio* (Paris, 1900 ff.), 20, cols. 721-728; Lupus, p. 62; Romuald. Sal., p. 412.

hemond.[40] During the course of the council, Roger was made the vassal of the pope, as his father had been before him, and received a banner in token of his investiture. [41] Bohemond, accompanied by his brother, now repeated in person the invitation which he had already extended to the pope through his messengers, and prevailed upon the pontiff to accompany him into his own possessions to consecrate Elias, the recently elected successor to Orso, archbishop of Bari, and to officiate at the transfer of the bones of St. Nicholas to a more fitting sanctuary. [42] From Melfi, Urban went, perhaps indirectly, and no doubt accompanied by Roger and Bohemond, to Venosa, where he issued a document on September 21. [43] Urban ordained Elias archbishop at Bari on September 30, and on the next day consecrated the shrine of St. Nicholas. [44] He was still at Bari on October 7, [45] and on the eleventh he was at Irani, [46] perhaps accompanied by Bohemond; and either be- fore or after the journey to Trani, he consecrated a church at Brindisi, [47] no doubt at Bohemond's request. On December 25, he was back in Rome. [48]

On August 19, 1090, Bohemond was in Taranto, and confirmed all grants in that city which had been made by Robert Guiscard to the Monastery of Monte Cassino. [49]

In May, 1091, Roger with the aid of Bohemond and of Count Roger with his Saracen army, besieged the long-rebellious city of Cosenza, and captured it late in June or in July. [50] In the same year, Oria revolted, and was besieged by Bohemond, but the citizens with the aid of Robert of Anzi attacked and routed the besieging army,

40. Joannes Barensis, p. 331.

41. Romuald. Sal, p. 412.

42. Joannes Barensis, p. 331; *Cod. dip. Bar.*, 1, pp. 61-63, 64-65.

43. Guillaume, p. 20.

44 The anonymous *Bari Chronicle* gives the dates. *An. Bar. Chron.*, p. 154. The letters of Urban and Elias, *Cod., dip. Bar.*, 1, pp. 62, 64, and the testimony of Lupus Protospatarius, p. 62, however, mention the consecration of the shrine before the ordination of the archbishop.

45. *Cod. dip. Bar.*, 1, pp. 61-63. The editors have incorrectly dated the letter October 5.

46. Jaffé—Loewenfeld, 5413.

47. Lupus, p. 62.

48. Jaffé—Loewenfeld, 5415.

49. Gattola, *Accessiones*, 1, pp. 205-206; *Chron. mon. Cas.*, pp. 764-765. A document of Bohemond's dated at Bari, December, 1090, is probably a forgery. *Cod. dip. Bar.*, 5, pp. 29-30.

50. The expedition returned in June, according to Malaterra, p. 596.

capturing its standards and baggage.[51] In November, 1091, Bohemond bestowed the *mundium* of a woman named Aza upon the Church of St. Nicholas,[52] and in the same month made another donation to the same church.[53]

On November 20, 1092, Bohemond with an Apulian count named William, attended Urban II at Anglona; on November 24, Urban was at Taranto, presumably on Bohemond's invitation.[54]

In August, 1093, Roger and Bohemond were with Urban at Monte Cassino, where they requested him to consecrate the Monastery of St. Mary of St. Banzi.[55] In October, Bohemond confirmed to Archbishop Elias, probably at Bari, a grant of the town of Bitritto, the tithes and the jurisdiction over the Jews and their debtors in Bari, a tract of land in Canale, the Church of St. Angelo *in monte Joannacii*, dominion over the prostitutes and two house in Noia.[56] In the same year, Bohemond gave his consent to a donation of a certain Geoffrey, son of Aitardus of Petrolla, to the Monastery of the Holy Trinity at Venosa.[57]

Toward the end of the year, Duke Roger became violently ill at Melfi with a sickness which the doctors could not diagnose, and it was not long before a rumour of his death spread throughout southern Italy and came to the ears of Bohemond, who was visiting his Calabrian possessions. Believing that his brother was dead, Bohemond seized his fortresses in Calabria, with the explanation that he intended to respect the rights of his brother's heirs, and that he was merely acting as their guardian. A number of Roger's less important vassals now revolted at the news of their suzerain's death, among them William of Grantmesnil, his brother-in-law, who promptly seized Rossano.

Informed eventually that his brother was not dead but was recovering from his illness and very probably overawed by the threatening attitude of Count Roger of Sicily who had come into Calabria to defend his nephew's interests, Bohemond hastened to Melfi, where he restored to his brother the fortresses he had seized. The duke's other rebellious vassals surrendered, presumably at this time, with the

51. Lupus, p. 62; Romuald. Sal., p. 412.

52. Putignani, 2, p. 312.

53. *Ibid.*, p. 341.

54. Mansi, 20, col. 684. A grant of Roger's to the Church of St. John of Aversa, dated in May of this year, and signed by Bohemond, is probably a forgery. *Regii Neapolitani archivii monumenta edita ac illustrata* (Naples, 1845-1861), 5, no. 455; di Meo, 8, p. 331.

55. Mansi, 20, cols. 643-644.

56. *Cod. dip. Bar.*, I, pp. 65-67.

57. Crudo, p. 188.

exception of William of Grantmesnil, who refused to return Rossano, and rejected the efforts of Roger of Sicily at mediation. As soon as his health permitted, Roger Borsa, with his uncle and Bohemond marched on Rossano, early in 1094, [58] and very promptly received its surrender, with the exception of the citadel, which was held by William's men. The town of Castrovillari surrendered after a siege of three weeks, and the rebellious William was forced to flee to Constantinople. [59]

In January, 1094, William, *catapan* of Bari, in the name of Bohemond, made a sale to the Church of St. Nicholas in Bari, [60] and in the following months carried on two somewhat similar transactions with the same church. [61]

We know nothing of Bohemond's activities in 1095, but the closing months of that year saw the meeting of the Council of Clermont and the preaching of the First Crusade, events of the greatest importance for the history of Europe, and the future of Bohemond, as well.

---

58. In January, 1094, Bohemond made a grant to the Church of St. Nicholas at Bari. Putignani, 2, p. 341. The expedition undoubtedly started after the document was issued.
59. Malaterra, pp. 597-598.
60. *Cod. dip. Bar.*, 5, pp. 35-36.
61. *Ibid.*, pp. 37-38, 38-40.

CHAPTER 4

The First Crusade:
To the Siege of Antioch

The preaching of the Crusade disclosed new prospects to the ambitious and dissatisfied Bohemond. Hemmed in as he was in Italy by his half-brother and uncle, he welcomed an undertaking which would make possible for him the aggrandizement in the East which he found impossible of attainment in his native land. So opportune for him was this unique expedition that William of Malmesbury thought that the whole idea of the Crusade had been conceived by Bohemond, in order that he might have a favourable opportunity to attack the Byzantine Empire. [1]

It is impossible to determine when the news of Clermont and of the preaching of the Crusade reached southern Italy and came to Bohemond's ears. Lupus Protospatarius notes in his chronicle a shower of meteors, which was seen throughout all Apulia on a Thursday night in April, 1095, that is, over half a year before the Council of Clermont, and then continues, "From that time on, the people of Gaul, and, indeed, of all Italy too, began to proceed with their arms to the Sepulchre of the Lord, bearing on their right shoulders the sign of the cross." [2] Even if Lupus is correct in his statements, it is obviously impossible to

---

1. Wil. Malm., 2, p. 390. Inspired principally by this statement, Palgrave imagined the fantastic theory that the Greek legates at Piacenza were really disguised agents of Bohemond, that Bohemond was the forger of the so-called *epistola spuria* of Alexius, and that Peter the Hermit was his tool. Sir Francis Palgrave, *The History of Normandy and England* (London, 1851-1864), 4.

2. Lupus, p. 62. The phenomenon of the falling stars was observed in France on the night of April 4. Heinrich Hagenmeyer, "*Chronologie de la Première Croisade et de l'histoire du royaume de Jérusalem,*" in the *Revue de l'Orient latin*, 1898-1911, 6-12, no. 6. (Cited as HCh.)

fix at all exactly the date of the departure of the first contingents from Italy. It is not improbable that the idea of the Crusade was brought up in March, 1095, at the Council of Piacenza, [3] and the news may have spread throughout Italy, so that there is nothing inherently impossible in Lupus' story. The remark of the author of the *Gesta Francorum* that the army of Peter the Hermit on its arrival in Constantinople found a number of "Lombards and Langobards," who had preceded it thither, seems to serve as a confirmation of Lupus' account. [4]

Even if we admit that the report of the departure of these early expeditions from Italy is unfounded, we may be sure that the news of Urban's undertaking was known in southern Italy not long after the Council of Clermont, for it is unthinkable that the pope should have neglected to inform Roger and Bohemond, his own vassal and *arrière-vassal*, with whom he had enjoyed rather close personal relations. A letter, similar to that which was directed by Urban to the princes and people of Flanders,[5] may have been sent to them, or legates have been dispatched to preach the Crusade in the south of Italy, just as they were sent to Genoa. [6]

Bohemond seems to have given little heed to the Crusade until the numerous bands of pilgrims, moving down through southern Italy to the Apulian sea-ports, convinced him that a really great movement was on foot. His decision to take the cross was arrived at undoubtedly only after careful consideration of the step, but it was announced to southern Italy in sudden and dramatic fashion. [7]

The siege of Amalfi, which had revolted from Duke Roger and set up a duke of its own, had resulted in the assembling about the walls of the city in July and August, 1096, of a large army under the command of the two Rogers and Bohemond. Taking advantage of this concentration of fighting-men, Bohemond, who had hitherto kept secret his design, appeared one day in August with the Crusaders' cross upon his shoulder, thus making it known to all that the oldest and ablest of

---

3. Bernoldus, *Chronicon*, in MGSS, 5, p. 462.

4. HG, p. 111.

5. Comte Paul Riant, *Inventaire critique des lettres historiques des croisades*, in the *Archives de l'Orient latin*, 1881, 1, p. 220.

6. Cafarus Genuensis, *De liberatione Orientis liber, Rec., Hist, occ.*, 5, p. 49; Jacobus de Voragine, *Chronicon*, in Muratori, RISS, 9, p. 31.

7. Even some of the contemporary or almost contemporary sources recognized that Bohemond's decision to go on the Crusade was determined by a desire for further conquests and not by religious zeal. Malaterra, p. 599; Wil. Malm., 2, p. 390; Anna, 2, pp. 32, 47.

the sons of Guiscard had decided to take the way to the Holy Land. A considerable portion of the army besieging Amalfi followed Bohemond's example, took the cross, and with him left the siege. The two Rogers, having seen their armies melt away before their eyes, raised the siege and returned home. [8]

Bohemond, after leaving Amalfi, returned to Apulia to prepare for the expedition.[9] Unfortunately, we know next to nothing of these preparations. In a document dated August, 1096, he extends to Guidelmus Flammengus, *catapan* of Bari, full right to sell or otherwise dispose of his possessions in Bari, evidence possibly of an attempt to raise money for his undertaking. [10] He seems to have appointed no regent for his possessions, but to have left them under the supervision of his local agents who acted in his name, and with whom he later probably attempted to keep in touch from his principality in the East. [11]

Constantinople had been appointed as the meeting place of the crusading armies before their entrance into Turkish territory, and for Bohemond to reach the imperial city, it was necessary for him to cross the Adriatic and then march east across the whole breadth of the Byzantine Empire in Europe. In view of the part which he had played in the Norman campaigns of 1081-1085, he may well have had serious doubts as to the kind of reception which he would receive in Greece. [12] We may assume with a considerable degree of probability that he dispatched legates to Alexius, informing him of his plans and assuring him of their friendly character long before he left Italy, and further that his legates returned from Constantinople with a favourable answer. [13] How else can we explain the fact that Bohemond dared to land on the Albanian coast in the autumn of 1096 and was allowed

---

8. Malaterra, p. 599; HG, pp. 147-152; Lupus, p. 62; *Annales Cavenses*, in MGSS, 3, p. 190. The *Gesta* represent Bohemond as first learning of the Crusade from passing pilgrims at the siege of Amalfi and then cutting his finest cloak into crosses which he distributes to the enthusiastic army. There can be little doubt of the unexpectedness of Bohemond's action; "*subito inspiratione*," says Lupus.

9. HG, p. 152.

10. *Cod. dip. Bar.*, 5, pp. 41-42. It must be noted, however, that another document issued by Bohemond in 1094, has almost the same content. *Cod. dip. Bar.*, 5, p. 37. There was, therefore, nothing unusual in this grant of 1096.

11. Chalandon, *Domination normande*, 1, p. 302.

12. Rad., p. 606.

13. The late and untrustworthy *Estoire de Jérusalem et d'Antioche*, in *Rec., Hist, occ.*, 5, pp. 627-628, tells of the sending of a delegation by Bohemond to Alexius to obtain a safe-conduct, an account, which, however incorrect its details, undoubtedly had some foundation in fact.

by Alexius' troops to pass unmolested into the interior?

It is impossible to arrive at a definite conclusion as to the size of the expedition which left Italy with Bohemond. According to Lupus Protospatarius, more than five hundred knights left the siege of Amalfi to join Bohemond. [14] To this number must be added the foot-soldiers, and those who took the cross in other places, combatants and non-combatants. Anna Comnena is inconsistent in her description of Bohemond's army; in her account of the beginning of the expedition, she refers to his "innumerable army," while later she remarks that his resources were slight and his army small, one of the smallest, in fact, of all the bands which made up the great crusading force. [15] Judging from the very prominent part which Bohemond played in the councils of the crusading leaders, we may be safe in assuming that his expedition must have been of a very considerable size.

Chief among Bohemond's followers was his nephew, Tancred, the son of Emma, Bohemond's half-sister, and Odo the Good Marquis. [16] Next to nothing is known of his life prior to his joining his uncle's army. A typical Norman in his bravery, his love of adventure, and his avarice, he was to prove a valuable lieutenant to Bohemond, even though he lacked the larger qualities of statecraft and generalship which his uncle possessed. [17] The sources also mention as members of the expedition Robert, the brother of Tancred, [18] Richard of the Principate and his brother Rainulf, sons of William Iron-Arm, and hence cousins of Bohemond, Rainulf's son Richard, Robert of Anzi, probably the same Robert who had routed Bohemond at the siege of Oria in 1091, Hermann of Canni, son of Humphrey de Hauteville and cousin of Bohemond, Robert of Sourdeval, Robert, the son of Tostan, Humphrey, the son of Ralph, Boello of Chartres, Albered of

14. Lupus, p. 62.

15. Anna, 2, pp. 40, 63-64. Albertus Aquensis, *Historia Hierosolymitana*, in *Rec., Hist, occ.,* 4, p. 312, estimates the size of Bohemond's army at 10,000 horsemen, in addition to a large number of foo-soldiers.

16 .Hagenmeyer has proved conclusively that Tancred was Bohemond's nephew and not his cousin, as has frequently been stated. Ekkehardus Uraugiensis abbas, *Hierosolymita*, edited by Heinrich Hagenmeyer (Tübingen, 1877), p. 329, n. 24. (Cited as HE.) Cf. F. de Saulcy, Tancrède, in *Bibliothèque de l'Ecole des Chartes*, 1842-1843, 4, pp. 301-315. Willermus Tyrensis, *Historia rerum in partibus transmarinis gestarum*, in *Rec., Hist, occ.,* 1, p. 80, calls Tancred's father "William the Good Marquis."

17. HG, p. 152; Rad., pp. 605-607. Sybel has an excellent character sketch of Tancred. Heinrich von Sybel, *Geschichte des ersten Kreuzzuges* (Leipzig, 1881), pp. 229-231.

18. Rad., p. 611.

Cagnano, Humphrey of Montescaglioso, Geoffrey *de Russinolo*, with his brothers, Gerard, bishop of Ariano, and the bishop of Russinolo,[19] Robert, the son of Gerard, who acted as Bohemond's constable, [20] Ralph the Red, [21] and Peter, bishop of Anagni. [22]

Bohemond's army, like all the other crusading armies, was undoubtedly composed of widely dissimilar elements, varying from the clergy and the very pious folk who went for the good of their souls and the discomfiture of the infidel to the unscrupulous adventurers who welcomed the Crusade as an opportunity for limitless fighting and plunder. There must have been many of this latter class in the army; Malaterra tells us that the persons who took the cross after Bohemond at Amalfi were the young men "who were anxious for something new, as is natural at that age." [23] From one point of view, Bohemond's army was the best prepared of all the crusading bands for such an expedition as the First Crusade was to be; for there were many men in it who had come into contact both with the Saracens in Sicily and the Greeks in southern Italy. If we may believe the author of the *Historie, belli sacri*, who seems to be well informed on south Italian affairs, both Tancred and Richard of the Principate knew Arabic,[24] and there may have been many more in the army who knew Arabic and Greek as well. We have already seen how well Bohemond's environment fitted him to be the leader of an expedition in the East.

Bohemond's army did not cross the Adriatic as a unit. One division left Italy some time before Bohemond's departure, with orders to await his crossing and the promise that he would indemnify them for any expenditures on their part caused by his delay. The advance guard seems to have landed at Durazzo, Avlona, and other Albanian sea-ports. [25] It is highly probable that the main body of the army under Bohemond, which left Italy late in October, 1096, did not leave from a single port, but took ship in smaller detachments in the various Apulian coast cities. [26] Bohemond landed at or near Avlona, and was joined on November I by that portion of his army which had

19. HG, pp. 153-155; HEp, p. 156; *Historia belli sacri* in *Rec., Hist, occ.*, 3, pp. 176, 189; *Chron. mon. Cas.*, p. 766; Alb., p. 316.

20. HG, p. 270; Rad., p. 668; Alb., p. 316.

21. HEp, p. 156.

22 . *Vita beati Petri episcopi Anagnini*, AASS, 3 Aug., 1, p. 238.

23. Malaterra, p. 599.

24. *Hist. bel. sacr.*, p. 198.

25. Alb., p. 312.

26. *An. Bar. Chron.*, p. 154.

preceded him. [27]

The launching of the Crusade and the arrival in the Byzantine Empire of the thousands of armed Westerners on their way to the Holy Land confronted Alexius with a most difficult problem. We shall probably never know with certainty whether or not Alexius appealed for aid against the Turks from Urban II, but if he did, he soon found himself in the position of Gibbon's Hindu shepherd who prayed for water and received a flood. Naturally suspicious of the designs of these turbulent and ambitious barbarians, above all of Bohemond and his Normans, and vexed and angered by the crimes and depredations of their undisciplined followers, whose "numbers surpassed the stars and sands," the *basileus*, his daughter tells us, was buffeted about by a sea of cares. [28] His first duty was, of course, to his empire, and he decided, if possible, to exploit the Franks for his own imperial ends. In accordance with this policy, he did all in his power to aid and to quicken the passage of the Crusaders through his possessions, establishing markets along the roads over which they travelled and supplying imperial officers and interpreters to facilitate the intercourse of the Westerners with the Greeks. At the same time, he attempted to protect his own subjects by establishing strong garrisons at strategic points, and by sending mobile forces to observe and follow the Crusaders' line of march. [29]

As a result of Alexius' policy, Bohemond encountered no resistance when he landed in Albania, nor did his forces experience any difficulty in buying food and wine at Avlona. [30] Probably soon after landing, Bohemond dispatched messengers to Constantinople to announce his arrival.[31]

Nothing is more obvious than Bohemond's desire to reassure the *basileus* by his actions of the friendliness of his motives. Conscious of the weight of suspicion and hatred which opposed him, he had come to the conclusion that he could not accomplish his own ends without winning the friendship, or at least allaying the suspicions, of the Greeks. His general policy, then, on the march to Constantinople was to prevent attacks upon the natives and to fall in as much as possible

---

27. *Hist, bel. sacr.*, p. 177; Anna, 2, pp. 39-40; Peter Matkovic, *Reisen durch die Balkanhalbinsel während des Mittelalters* (Vienna, 1880), p. 37.
28. Anna, 2, p. 272.
29. Anna, 2, pp. 31-32, 273.
30. HG, p. 156.
31. HG, p. 163.

with the wishes of Alexius and his representatives. So we find him, shortly after the collection of his forces in Albania, urging them not to ravage the country through which they were about to pass;[32] somewhat later, on the march, angrily vetoing a plan of Tancred and some of the other leaders to attack a fortified town; and then, at the request of Greek officials, ordering the return of cattle which had been seized by members of his army.[33]

Leaving the coast, Bohemond's army moved eastward through the regions which he and his father had invaded fifteen years before, marching through a country of "great plenty, from village to village, from city to city, from fortress to fortress," until it reached Castoria, where it spent Christmas Day.[34] The sight of the great fortress must have called up varying emotions in Bohemond's mind, and it is quite evident that the natives of the region also remembered the Norman campaigns of 1082-1083, for they refused to sell food to the Crusaders, thinking that they had come to invade and devastate the country. Bohemond's troops, thereupon, seized the cattle, horses, asses, and whatever else they could find.[35]

From Castoria, the expedition marched eastward into the district of Pelagonia, where it sacked and burned a settlement of heretics, together with the inhabitants. Continuing its way, undoubtedly over the ancient Via Egnatia, it reached the Vardar River about the middle of February, where it camped for a few days. While about to cross the river on February 18, the Norman rear guard was suddenly attacked by a body of Turcopoles and Petchenegs. Tancred, at the head of some Norman troops, hastily recrossed the river and routed the enemy, capturing a number of them and taking them before Bohemond. To his indignant questions as to why they had attacked his army, they could only answer that they were in the service of the *basileus* and that they had merely obeyed his commands. In accordance with Bohemond's pacificatory policy, they were finally allowed to depart unharmed.[36] It seems probable that the attack was caused by plundering on the part of Bohemond's troops, an episode which the Western sources have not unnaturally failed to mention.

---

32. *Ibid.*, pp. 156-158.
33. *Ibid.*, p. 166.
34. Matkovic, p. 38, conjectures that Bohemond marched up the left bank of the Wojutza to Tepelena, from there to Argyrokastro, and thence through the valley of the Drin to Castoria.
35. HG, pp. 158-159.
36. HG, pp. 159-163; Rad., pp. 607-610.

Sometime after the attack on the Vardar, the legates whom Bohemond had sent to Constantinople returned in company with a Greek official, who had been instructed to act as the guide of the expedition until it reached Constantinople. Thereafter the Crusaders did not want for food, although the inhabitants of the cities which they passed refused to allow them to enter the gates. On April 1, the army reached Ruskoï, where it was well received by the inhabitants, and whence Bohemond, turning over the command of the expedition to Tancred set out for Constantinople with a small retinue at the request of Alexius. [37]

In the meantime, two other leaders had made their way to Constantinople. Hugh of Vermandois, the vainglorious and not overly courageous brother of Philip I of France, had been captured by Alexius' officials on landing on the Albanian coast and conducted to Constantinople, [38] while Godfrey of Bouillon, duke of Lower Lorraine; a brave and capable soldier, at the head of an army of considerable size, had made his way through Hungary and the Balkans, and had arrived before Constantinople on December 23. [39]

Alexius, unwilling to allow the Westerners to pass over into territory once ruled and still claimed by the Greeks, without assuring himself of their willingness and intention to respect his claims, hoped to realize this end by exacting from them the western oath of vassalage. Hugh of Vermandois, won over by the gifts of Alexius, took the oath without much hesitation, [40] but Godfrey, unwilling to commit himself, remained with his army in the suburbs, carrying on protracted negotiations with the *basileus* and awaiting the arrival of Bohemond and the other leaders, with whose aid he hoped to be able to offer a successful resistance to Alexius' demands.

Alexius, however, sent troops to guard the roads from Athyra to Philea, and to intercept any messages which might pass between Godfrey and Bohemond. As a result, Bohemond undoubtedly remained ignorant throughout his march of what was taking place at Constantinople. Albert of Aachen's account of the sending by Bohemond of legates to Godfrey suggesting a joint attack on the capitol is unques-

---

37. HG, pp. 163-167; Anna, 2, p. 60; Rad., pp. 611-613.
38. HG, pp. 137-139; Anna, 2, pp. 36-39; Fulcherius Carnotensis, *Historia Hierosolymitana*, edited by Heinrich Hagenmeyer (Heidelberg, 1913), pp 154-156. (Cited as HF.)
39. HG, pp. 140-141.
40. HG, p. 140; Anna, 2, p. 39.

tionably untrue, in view of the policy which Bohemond had adopted toward Alexius. Equally false is Anna's assertion that Bohemond and the other leaders had conspired to capture Constantinople. Godfrey, after an indecisive skirmish with the imperial troops on April 2, finally consented to take the oath which was demanded of him, and became the vassal of Alexius. [41]

In spite of the friendliness which Bohemond had consistently displayed throughout his march to Constantinople, Alexius still mistrusted and feared his designs, [42] and it must have been with some trepidation that he saw the entry of the son of Guiscard into the capital. He, nevertheless, received him graciously, inquired politely about his journey and where he had left his army, and then spoke of the Battles of Durazzo and Larissa. Bohemond, probably abashed by the turn the conversation had taken, protested that if he had been Alexius' enemy in the past, he was now his friend, and intimated that he was not averse to taking the oath of vassalage.

Alexius, however, suggested that they postpone the matter until Bohemond had rested from his journey, and dismissed him to the Cosmidium, north of the city, where quarters had been made ready for him. According to Anna, Alexius had food prepared for Bohemond, but the Norman, fearing an attempt to poison him, would not touch it and gave orders to his own cooks to take the raw meat which Alexius had also provided and to prepare it for him. He gave the cooked food, which Alexius' servants had placed before him, to some of his attendants, and inquired on the next day concerning their health. On learning that the food had not affected them, Bohemond confessed that he had feared treachery on Alexius' part. [43]

Bohemond willingly took the oath of homage which Alexius demanded of him. [44] The statement of the *Gesta Francorum* that Bohemond was induced to become the vassal of the *basileus* on the latter's promise to bestow upon him the region about Antioch, fifteen days' journey in extent in one direction and eight in the other, is undoubt-

---

41. HG, pp. 140-147; Anna, 2, pp. 46-55; Alb., pp. 299-312. I have followed Anna rather than Albert, who places these events in January. Kugler's criticism of Anna's account has been very well answered by Chalandon. Bernard Kugler, *Peter der Eremite und Albert von Aachen*, in the *Historische Zeitschrift*, 1880, 14, pp. 34 ff.; *Kaiser Alexius und Albert von Aachen*, in *Forschungen zur deutschen Geschichte*, 1883, 23, pp. 495 ff.; Chalandon, *Alexis*, p. 179, n. 4.

42. Anna, 2, pp. 60, 65.

43 *Ibid*, pp. 61-63.

44. *Ibid.*, p. 63; HG, pp. 171-172; Alb., p. 312.

edly false, for during his later wars with Alexius, Bohemond seems never to have urged the grant as a justification for his possession of Antioch. After the capture of Antioch, however, Bohemond may have told this story to his own followers, in order to obtain their support in his attempt to maintain possession of the city.

Bohemond was rewarded with the usual gifts which Alexius bestowed upon the crusading leaders. According to Anna, he was introduced unexpectedly into a room in the palace which had been filled almost to overflowing with gold, silver, rich garments, and other treasures, where, struck by the sight of so much wealth, the greedy Norman exclaimed, "If I had such riches as these, I should long ago have been master of many lands." He was overjoyed when the whole contents of the room were offered to him, but later with true Frankish fickleness, sent back the gifts to the *basileus*: Alexius, understanding the nature of the man with whom he was dealing, ordered them returned to Bohemond, who accepted and kept them. [45]

We also learn from Anna the remarkable fact that Bohemond asked Alexius for the office of grand domestic of the Orient, but received only an evasive answer. [46] The story is not impossible; Norman adventurers had held responsible offices in the Byzantine Empire before this, [47] and such an appointment might have fallen in very well with Bohemond's plans, if he already had designs upon the Empire. What his exact plans were and precisely what end he had in view when he took the cross, beyond the very general end of personal aggrandizement, we shall probably never know. Not improbably he had already fixed his ambitions upon the possession of Antioch.

It is to be regretted that the terms of the oath of vassalage which Bohemond and the other leaders took to Alexius have not been preserved in their original form. The sources, however, which mention the terms, agree remarkably with one another, and allow us to be reasonably sure of at least the principal items of the agreement. The leaders of the crusading armies became the vassals of Alexius, and promised to restore to him whatever lands or cities they captured which had once belonged to the Empire, and which were now in the hands of its enemies.

---

45. Anna, 2, pp. 63-64; Alb., p. 313.
46. *Ibid*, p. 65.
47. Gustave Schlumberger, *Deux chefs normands des armées byzantines au XIe siècle* in the *Revue historique*, 1881, 16, pp. 289-303; Francesco Brandileone, *I Primi Normanni d'Italia in Oriente*, in the *Rivista storica italiana*, 1884, 1, pp. 227-251.

We do not know unfortunately what agreement was made as to what constituted the original boundaries of the Empire. William of Tyre thinks that the Franks promised to return all their conquests north of Jerusalem. [48] According to Gislebert of Mons, who wrote early in the thirteenth century, all conquests made in the territory up to and including Antioch were to be restored. [49] It will be evident from subsequent events that the crusading leaders pledged themselves to restore at least as much territory as Gislebert has indicated. Alexius, for his part, engaged himself to give military aid to the Crusaders on land and sea, and eventually to assume command in person of the Greek forces cooperating with the Franks, to furnish them with markets where they could buy food during their campaign, to make reparation for all losses sustained by the Franks, and to guarantee the safety of pilgrims passing through the Byzantine Empire. [50] According to William of Tyre, Alexius also awarded the Crusaders the right to all the spoils in the cities which they captured. [51]

Bohemond's efforts to placate and reassure Alexius are obvious in the days which follow. Count Robert of Flanders, Bohemond's brother-in-law, who arrived in Constantinople some time after him, took the oath which Alexius required, but Count Raymond of Toulouse, a hot-headed, fanatical, avaricious, old soldier, refused to take the oath, and the news that his army of *Provençals* which he had left at Rodosto had been attacked by the Greek troops only confirmed him in his decision. Alexius explained that Raymond's troops had been guilty of pillaging the country about their camp, and had been attacked for that reason; he was ready, nevertheless, to give the count satisfaction for the attack, and put forward Bohemond (of all men!) as a pledge for the reparation.

The case was arbitrated and decided against Raymond, who now began to plan an attack on Alexius, but the opposition of Godfrey and Robert of Flanders, and the threat of Bohemond that he would support the *basileus* if Raymond attacked him or delayed taking the oath, forced him to give up the idea and take a modified form of the oath. He swore by his life and honour that he would neither himself nor

48. WT, p. 307.
49. Gislebertus, *Chronicon Hanoniense*, in MGSS, 21, p. 504.
50. HG, p. 173; HE, pp. 143-144; Anna, 2, pp. 54-55; Alb., pp. 311, 321, 434, 501, 652; *Epistula Boemundi . . . ad universes Christi fideles*, in HEp, p. 154; WT, p. 307; Matthieu d'Edesse, *Extraits de la chronique de*, in *Rec., Doc. arm.*, 1, p. 27.
51. WT, pp. 127-128.

through the agency of anyone else seize any of the possessions of the *basileus*. As for taking the oath of homage, he said, he would have none of it even at the peril of his head. "Wherefore," writes his chronicler, "the emperor bestowed but paltry largess upon him." [52]

Successful as he had been in forcing Raymond of Toulouse to a compromise with Alexius, Bohemond was less fortunate in dealing with the leaders of his own forces, which, in the meantime had reached Constantinople and passed over into Asia, for Tancred and Richard of the Principate stole out of the city in secret and rejoined the army on the other side of the Bosphorus in order to avoid taking the oath of homage. Bohemond, on learning of his nephew's flight, could only assure Alexius that he would eventually obtain Tancred's submission. [53]

The growing ascendancy of Bohemond among the crusading chiefs is borne witness to by the fact that it was he who remained behind in Constantinople to negotiate with Alexius regarding the provisioning of the armies which were now pressing on to besiege Nicea and it was Bohemond who eventually succeeded in having food brought to the hungry troops. [54]

Nicea, capital of the Sultanate of Rum and the most important city in Kilij Arslan's empire, had been a menace to Constantinople ever since its capture by the Turks, and it was due probably to the requests of Alexius rather than to the fact that the capture of the city was necessary to the successful prosecucution of their campaign that the Crusaders besieged it. Since the Lake of Nicea, which bordered the Turkish capital on the west, [55] prevented the Crusaders, whose forces had been augmented by the contingents of Robert of Normandy and Stephen of Blois, from investing the city completely, Alexius acceded to the request of the Crusaders for a fleet of ships and had a number of vessels dragged overland to the Lake of Nicea, where they were filled with Turcopoles under the command of Manuel Butumites, the imperial representative with the Prankish armies.

Alexius also dispatched at the same time a division of Greek troops

---

52. Raimundus de Aguilers, *Historia Francorum qui ceperunt Iherusalem*, in *Rec., Hist, occ.*, 3, pp. 236-238; HG, pp. 173-175.

53. HG, pp. 175-176; Rad., pp. 613-615; Alb., p. 313.

54. HG, pp. 176, 178.

55. For the topography of Nicea, see Colmar, Freiherr von der Goltz, *Anatolische Ausflüge* (Berlin, n.d.), pp. 399-460; Vital Cuinet, *La Turquie d'Asie* (Paris, 1892), 4, pp. 73-74.

under Taticius and Tzitas. The Turks chose to surrender to the Greeks rather than to the Franks, and on the morning of June 19, just as the Crusaders had begun a fresh attack upon the city, Butumites appeared upon the walls, and elevating the imperial standards, proclaimed amid the blowing of trumpets the name of his sovereign, Alexius Comnenus. Fearing a sack of the city, the Byzantine general allowed the Crusaders to enter the gates only at intervals and in small groups. [56]

The precautions of the Greeks caused the liveliest dissatisfaction among the Franks, who had hoped to plunder the city, and it was only by the persuasion of Bohemond that the most of the leaders were induced to accept the invitation of Alexius to attend him at Pelecanum, where he wished to thank and reward them for their efforts and undoubtedly hoped that he might obtain the oath of homage from those leaders who had thus far avoided taking it. He was successful in his undertaking, for all the leaders who had not already become his vassals took the oath, with the exception of Tancred, who, according to Anna, protested that he owed fealty to Bohemond alone. He finally consented to take the oath if Alexius rewarded him fittingly, and after a stormy scene between him and George Palaeologus, who had showed his disapproval of the Norman's avarice, a scene in which Bohemond tried to placate his nephew, Tancred finally took the oath. [57]

The fact that Alexius had not given over Nicea to the Crusaders to sack made it necessary for him to recompense them for the loss of their plunder, and rich gifts were bestowed on the leaders, while the poor folk of army received large alms in the shape of copper coins. [58] Nevertheless, some of the nobles were dissatisfied with the treatment they had received at the hands of the *basileus*, to judge from the statement in the letter of Anselm of Ribemont, "Some departed with good feeling, others otherwise." The feeling of the *Provençals* against Alexius was especially violent, and Raymond of Agiles writes in his usual racy style, "After the city had been taken, Alexius gave the army such cause for gratitude, that as long as he shall live, the people will forever curse him and proclaim him traitor." [59]

56. HG, pp. 178-192; Raim., pp. 239-240; HF, pp. 181-189; Anna, 2, pp. 70-81; Alb., pp. 318-328; *Epistula I Stephani comitis Carnotensis ad Adelam uxorem suam*, in HEp, pp. 139-140; *Epistula I Anselmi de Ribodimonte ad Manassem archiepiscopum Remorum*, in HEp, p. 144; Rad., pp. 617-618.

57. *Ep. I Steph.*, p. 140; Anna, 2, pp. 82-83; Rad., pp. 618-619; Ralph of Caen thinks that Tancred did not take the oath of vassalage.

58. *Ep. I Steph.*, p. 140; *Ep. I Anselm.*, p. 145; HG, pp. 194-195; HF, pp. 188-189.

59. Raim., p. 240.

Anxious to take advantage of the capture of Nicea and to retake the north-eastern portions of Asia Minor, Alexius postponed his participation in the Franks' campaign, and sent with them instead a Greek force under Taticius, the grand *primicerius*, who because of his Turkish descent, was likely to prove a valuable adviser to the Crusaders in their campaign against the Seljuks. According to Gislebert of Mons, there were only three thousand troops in the Greek contingent. [60] It was undoubtedly small, to judge from the in frequency with which it is mentioned in the Western sources. Even had his agreement with the Franks not necessitated the sending of a contingent of Greek troops with them, Alexius would undoubtedly have done so in order to garrison the cities which the Franks captured and restored to the Empire.[61]

The various divisions of the crusading army left Nicea at different times, and after convening again at the Gallus River, set out early on the morning of June 29 on the long march across Asia Minor. Daylight found the army separated into two groups, the troops of Bohemond, Robert of Normandy, and Stephen of Blois marching over one road, and those of Godfrey, Raymond, Hugh, and Robert of Flanders over another to the north and east of that followed by the Normans, the separation being either the result of a blunder or of a realization of the difficulty of feeding so large an army advancing over a single route. [62]

On the evening of June 30, scouts of Bohemond's army announced the presence of enemy forces ahead, and they returned again next morning with the news that the Turks were preparing for battle. Bohemond, who seems to have been in command of all the Norman forces, gave the order to dismount and to pitch camp near a swamp, and then exhorted his men to fight bravely against the enemy. [63] Not long afterwards, the Franks beheld the first charges of the Turkish cavalry and the beginning of the battle which has gone down into history

---

60. Anna, 1, p. 199. The Chanson of Antioch makes Taticius the nephew of Alexius. *La chanson d'Antioche*, edited by Paulin Paris (Paris, 1848), 1, p. 77. Raymond of Agiles says that he had lost his nose and his virtue as well. Raim., p. 245, Guibert of Nogent says that he used a gold nose in place of his own which had been cut off. Guibertus Novigentus, *Historia quae dicitur Gesta Dei per Francos*, in *Rec., Hist, occ.*, 4, p. 175; Gislebertus, p. 504.

61. Anna, 2, p. 83; Petrus Tudebodus, *Historia de Hierosolymitano itinere*, in *Rec., Hist, occ.*, 3, p. 41.

62. HG, pp. 195-197; *Ep. I, Anselm.*, p. 145; Alb., pp. 328-329; Rob. Mon., p. 759; Rad., pp. 620-621.

63 .HF, pp. 190-192; HG, p. 109.

as the Battle of Dorylaeum, but which was, in reality, probably fought at Inonnii or Bozüyük. [64]

Unable to withstand the Turkish attack, the Normans fell back on their camp, which had already been attacked from the rear by the Turkish horsemen. [65] Realizing that his whole army was in a serious plight, Bohemond sent to Godfrey and Raymond for aid. Valuable time seems to have been lost in getting into communication with the northern army, but the reinforcements arrived in time to save the Normans from disaster. Joining forces, the Crusaders hastily drew up a new line of battle, while Adhemar of Puy, the papal legate, began a flanking movement against the Turks, who fled almost at the first on-slaught, hotly pursued by the Franks, and leaving behind them a great amount of spoil. The victory was complete, and the military power of Kilij Arslan broken for some time to come. [66]

The further resistance of the Turks to the advance of the Cru-saders through Asia Minor and Armenia was slight and ineffectual. A detachment of Turks, which the Franks encountered near Heraclea, was routed by the spirited charges of Bohemond and his men. [67] Ru-mours of the presence of a Turkish army which came to the ears of the Crusaders near Plastentia failed to materialize, and Bohemond, who had left the main army to seek the Turks, rejoined the expedition at Marasch without having met the enemy forces. [68]

It was during the march through Asia Minor that we encounter the first definite evidence of Bohemond's designs upon Antioch. At Heraclea, Tancred and a group of Normans left the army and marched southeast into Cilicia, with the intention of securing control of the strategically important lands of Cilicia and northern Syria, outlying portions of the future principality of Antioch. With him went Bald-win, brother of Godfrey of Bouillon, with a force of Lotharingians, the presence of this body being undoubtedly an attempt of the Loth-aringian party to checkmate the plan for Norman aggrandizement,

64. Von der Goltz, pp. 456-457.

65. HF, pp. 194-197.

66. HG, pp. 197-205; HF, pp. 197-199; Raim., p. 240; Rad., pp. 625-629; Anna, 2, pp. 84-85; *Ep. I Anselm.*, p. 145; *Epistula Boamundi, Raimundi comitis s. Aegidii, Godefridi ducis Lotharingiae, Roberti comitis Flandrensis, Eustachii comitis Boloniae ad Urbanum II,* in HEp, pp. 161-162; Alb., pp. 331 ff. For a description of the whole battle, see Otto Heermann, *Die Gefechtsführung abendländischer Heere im Orient in der Epoche des ersten Kreuszuges,* Dissertation (Marburg, 1888), pp. 5-24.

67. HG, pp. 214-215; HF, pp. 204-205; Anna, 2, p. 85.

68. HG, p. 230.

and to gain their own share of the spoils.

After quarrelling with Baldwin over the disposition of Tarsus, to which they both laid siege, Tancred left the Lotharingians, marched eastward and secured possession of the important cities of Adana and Mamistra. [69] After capturing Tarsus and leaving a garrison there, Baldwin followed Tancred to Mamistra, where the armies of the two leaders engaged in a battle, in which the Normans were defeated. [70] Tancred then seems to have gone into Syria, where he captured a great number of fortresses in the region of Antioch; it is impossible to identify many of them, but the Port of St. Simeon, Alexandretta, Artasium or Artah, and probably Balana and Baghras were among the number.[71] Baldwin rejoined the crusading army at Marasch only to leave it to found the Latin county of Edessa. [72]

Events had already disclosed that Bohemond was to have a rival in his designs upon Antioch, for Raymond of Toulouse, hearing at Genksu that Antioch had been evacuated by its garrison, sent forward a detachment of his forces to seize the city. On approaching Antioch, they learned that Antioch was still defended by the Turks, and the *Provençals* contented themselves with capturing a number of fortresses in the vicinity. [73]

The actions of the Normans, the Lotharingians, and the *Provençals* were quite typical of the conduct of the leaders in general. As the army approached northern Syria, the scramble of the crusading nobles for fortresses and territory began. "Everyone wished to make his own fortune; no one thought of the public weal," writes Raymond of Agiles. [74]

As the Crusaders drew near to Antioch, a division arose in their councils. One group, no doubt including Taticius, was in favour of postponing the attack on Antioch and of awaiting the spring and the arrival of the *basileus* and reinforcements from the West, in view of the fact that the army had been depleted by the necessity of garrisoning the fortresses which it had captured; the other group, including Raymond of Toulouse, and undoubtedly Bohemond, argued in favour of

---

69. HG, pp. 216-224; Rad., pp. 630-636; Alb., pp. 343 ff.

70. Rad., pp. 635-639; Alb., pp. 349-350.

71. Rad., pp. 639-641; Alb., p. 357; Kamal-ad-Din, *Extraits de l'histoire d'Alep*, in *Rec., Hist, or.*, 3, p. 578.

72. HF, pp. 206-208.

73. HG, pp. 231-234.

74. Raim., p. 242.

beginning the siege immediately. [75] The view of the latter party was accepted, and in October, the army entered the plain of northern Syria, and after being joined by Tancred at Artah, marched southwest on Antioch. [76]

On October 20, the advance-guard of the army attacked and routed a Turkish force at the so-called Iron Bridge over the Orontes River, and on the evening of the same day, Bohemond, not to be anticipated by any other of the leaders, pushed ahead with four thousand troops, and encamped before the walls of Antioch. The rest of the army, which had spent the night in camp on the Orontes, joined him on the following day, October 21, 1097, and began the siege of the city." [77]

75. Raim., p. 241.
76. Alb., p. 362.
77 HG, pp. 239-241; *Ep. I Anselm.*, p. 145; Alb., pp. 362-365; HChr, no. 203.

CHAPTER 5

The First Crusade:
The Siege of Antioch and After

Antioch, once "Antioch the Glorious," and still one of the great cities of the Eastern world, had been captured by the Arabs in 638, [1] recaptured by the generals of Nicephorus Phocas in 969, [2] and in 1085 had fallen into the hands of the Seljukian Turks. [3] The magnificent fortress had been one of the masterpieces of Byzantine military engineering, and its strength had in no way decreased during the twelve years of Turkish occupation.

The city, which lay half in the plain which skirted the southern bank of the Orontes River, and half on the rugged slopes of the Casian Range, was surrounded by a great wall, in exposed positions a double wall, wide enough for a chariot to be drawn over it, and broken at varying intervals by huge three-storied towers, some sixty feet in height, which commanded the walls and the ground at their base as well. [4] Additional security was afforded the city by the Orontes which washed a portion of the northern and western walls, and to the south and east the mountains, up which the city walls ran in dizzying fashion, performed a similar function, while to the north an extent of marshy land, wedged in between the Orontes and the walls, made difficult an attack from that direction.

---

1. A. Müller, *Der Islam im Morgen-und Abendland* (Berlin, 1885-1887), I, p. 259.

2. Gustave Schlumberger, *Nicéphore Phocas* (Paris, 1890), pp. 706-726.

3. G. F. Hertzberg, *Geschichte der Byzantiner und des osmanischen Reiches bis gegen Ende des sechszehnten Jahrhunderts* (Berlin, 1883), p. 275.

4. How many towers there were it is impossible to say definitely. There were probably between three and four hundred. Richard Forster, *Antiochia am Orontes*, in *Jahrbuch des kaiserlichen deutschen archäologischen Instituts*, 1897, 12, pp. 142-143.

The walls were pierced by five large gates: St. Paul's Gate to the east; next, the Dog's Gate, opening on the marshes; the Duke's Gate, so-called by the Crusaders after Godfrey of Bouillon, whose army lay near it; and the Bridge Gate, leading to the bridge which spanned the Orontes, all three opening to the north in the order named; and last, St. George's Gate to the west.[5] In addition, there were numerous postern gates opening on to the mountains, through which messengers and spies might be sent out or food introduced.

The city walls included, or rather skirted the ridges of, three large hills which rose in the southern portion of the town; the middle hill was capped by a powerful citadel, an integral part of the walls, but otherwise unapproachable from the lower city except by a single narrow path, and fortified in addition by a precipice which was almost sheer to the east and north,[6]

The city proper, which covered only a fraction of the space within the walls, lay in the northern portion of the *enceinte*, surrounded by its gardens and orchards,—a pleasant place, one may believe, shaded from the eastern sun by the mountains, and echoing with the incessant ripple of the springs and rivulets which trickled down from the hills.[7] In the upper city, which lay terraced on the slopes, were baths heated with myrtle wood and gardens from which one might look out over the fertile levels of the Orontes.[8] Time and the hand of the barbarian, says Joannes Phocas, had extinguished something of its prosperity,[9] but the bazaars still drove a roaring trade in silks, for which the city was famous and their counters still displayed wares from all parts of the East.[10]

Altogether Antioch was one of the most formidable fortresses the world had yet seen. Raymond of Agiles exclaims, "So fortified was it with walls and towers and barbicans, that it had no need to fear the assault of any machine or the attack of any man, not even if all mankind were to come together against it,"[11] and Stephen of Blois writes home to his wife:

We found the great city of Antioch incredibly strong and im-

5. WT, p. 173.

6. *Ibid.*, pp. 235-236; Raim., p. 242.

7. WT, p. 169; Ibn Haukal, Ibn Butlân and Idrisi in Guy Le Strange, *Palestine under the Moslems* (Boston, 1890).

8. Ibn Butlân.

9. Joannes Phocas, *Pilgrimage in the Holy Land* (London, 1896)

10. Gustave Schlumberger, *Renaud de Châtillon* (Paris, 1898).

11. Raim., p. 242.

pregnable. [12]

There were only two possible ways of capturing the city, by starvation or by treachery. The Crusaders were to try both plans in turn.

The city, as we have seen, could be attacked conveniently by a besieging army only from the north and east, and it was in this region south of the Orontes that the Crusaders encamped. Bohemond took up his position to the east of Antioch in the hilly district before St. Paul's Gate, while the other Normans, the Flemish, and the French lay to his right. The *Provençals* and the Lotharingians pitched camp in the wedge of land between the walls and the river, Raymond observing the Dog's Gate, and Godfrey the Duke's Gate. [13] It will thus be apparent that only three of the five principal city gates were blockaded, and the Bridge Gate and St. Paul's Gate still permitted the Turks to enter or leave the city as they pleased.

The Crusaders realized themselves the imperfection of their siegering, but considerations of prudence kept them from dividing their forces so early in the siege and sending a portion of them across the Orontes to blockade the other two gates. The army had been weakened by the necessity of garrisoning the neighbouring towns and fortresses which had fallen an easy prey to the attacks of the Crusaders. [14] "Know for certain," writes Anselm of Ribemont to Manasses, archbishop of Reims, "that we have gained for the Lord two hundred cities and fortresses." [15] The ambitions and energies of the leaders during the first few weeks after their arrival were bent more on the capture of towns and castles in the surrounding country than on pushing the siege of Antioch. [16]

For two weeks after the beginning of the siege, the Crusaders carried on their operations only half-heartedly. Life was too pleasant in the fertile plain of Antioch with its apple orchards and vineyards heavy

---

12. *Ep. II Steph.*, in HEp, p. 150. For the description of Antioch, see also HG, pp. 397-399; HF, pp. 217-218; Rad., pp. 641-642; Le Strange, p. 367-377; Aboulféda, *Géographie* (Paris, 1848-1883), 2, pt. 2, p. 35; Bertrandon de la Broquière, *Le Voyage d'Outremer* (Paris, 1892), pp. 84-85; Forster, pp. 103-149; Oman, pp. 527-529; Emmanuel Guillaume Rey, *Étude sur les monuments de l'architecture militaire des croisés en Syrie et dans l'île de Chypre* (Paris, 1871), pp. 183-204; E. S. Bouchier, *A Short History of Antioch, 300 B.C.,-A.D. 1268* (Oxford, 1921), ch. 1.

13. Alb., pp. 365-366; Rad., p. 642; HG, pp. 242-243.

14. *Ep. II Steph.*, p. 151, According to Kamal-ad-Din, p. 578, many of the towns in northern Syria had revolted and slain their Turkish garrisons.

15. *Ep. I Anselm.*, p. 145.

16. Rad., p. 650; Raim., p. 242.

with grapes. [17] As for the enemy, they kept behind their walls and left the Christians unmolested in their carelessly guarded camps. Only the Syrians and Armenians, who had been expelled from Antioch by Yagi Siyan, the Turkish commander, or who were acting as his spies, came out of the city or from the towns and villages of the neighbourhood, and visited the camp of the Crusaders, begging Bohemond to persist in the siege and selling provisions to the Westerners. [18]

Some of them carried back military information to Yagi Siyan. Bohemond, we are told, put a stop to the espionage by ordering a number of Turkish prisoners to be brought out and killed about supper time and large fires to be kindled, at the same time ordering his servants to say to all who asked that the crusading leaders had decided to kill and eat as many of the enemy and his spies as they could capture. The ruse succeeded, says William of Tyre, and the spies fled in terror, spreading throughout the country this new tale of Frankish ferocity. [19]

Bohemond, it is possible, may already have been bent on obtaining Antioch. He had now seen with his own eyes the Syrian metropolis, after Constantinople, the finest city that he knew, for Rome of the eleventh century was no great place; and his men already held some of the prosperous Cilician cities and many of the villages and fertile districts of northern Syria. The value of the country was so obvious that he may have fixed his appetite upon it early in the siege but there is no definite evidence of the fact to be found in the sources. Whatever his plans may have been, we may be sure that they could not possibly have possessed at this period the definiteness which Kugler has ascribed to them, that is, the design of founding a principality which was eventually to absorb Palestine.[20]

Although the crusading chiefs chose Stephen of Blois as leader of the army during the siege,[21] the conceited Frenchman was little more than a figurehead, his election being due to his wealth and to his lack of territorial ambitions in the East rather than to his ability, while the energy, resourcefulness, and military talents of Bohemond made him the real leading spirit in the camp of the Crusaders. The serious illness of Godfrey and of Raymond and the repeated absences of Robert of

17. HG, p. 243.
18. *Hist. bel. sacr.*, p. 186; HG, pp. 244-245; Ibn el-Athîr, *Extraits de la chronique intitulée Kamal-Altevarykh*, in *Rec., Hist, or.*, 1, p. 192.
19. WT, pp. 189-190.
20. Bernhard Kugler, *Boemund und Tankred, Fürsten von Antiochien* (Tübingen, 1862), pp. 1-5.
21. *Ep. II Steph.*, p. 149; HG, p. 353; Raim., p. 258.

Normandy, who stole away to Laodicea to enjoy the pleasures of that Levantine seaport, threw upon Bohemond a large part of the responsibility for the siege. No wonder then that the Turks within the city looked upon him as the real leader of the Christian army. [22]

The Mohammedan powers of northern Syria were in no position to offer a very stern resistance to the invasion of the Westerners, because of the almost incessant strife between the virtually independent *emirs* of Antioch, of Aleppo, of Damascus, and of Homs. The beginning of the siege, however, compelled Yagi Siyan to lay aside any feelings of *amour propre* and to call upon the other *emirs* for aid. [23] At the same time, in the third week of the siege, the Turks began a series of sudden sorties from the city, issuing from the Bridge Gate to harass the Christian army, or stealing out from the posterns to waylay pilgrims who had wandered away from the camp. [24]

Equally serious was the damage which the Crusaders suffered from the persistent attacks of the Turks from Harem, a fortress some three hours to the east of Antioch on the road to Aleppo. An expedition under Bohemond undertook about the middle of November to put a check upon these raids. On coming into contact with a Turkish force from Harem, the advance guard of the Normans fell back upon the main body of the expedition. The Turks, lured into the ambush, were attacked by Bohemond's troops, many of them were killed, and a number were taken captive and beheaded before the walls of Antioch.[25]

In the efforts to obtain provisions for the army, Bohemond also stands out as the most important figure. By December the Crusaders had almost exhausted the food supplies in the district about Antioch, and the prices of food rose steadily; in spite of the limited amounts of food brought by the Greek ships to Laodicea and the Port of St. Simeon under the terms of their agreement, and the supplies which the Armenians sold to the starving Christians at exorbitant rates (the Armenian touch), the suffering was very great. The presence of Turkish bands in the surrounding country made it dangerous to go far afield and even the journey to the ports was a perilous business to be undertaken only by a strong armed party. [26] To add to the misery of the

---

22. See *infra.*, this chapter.
23. *Ep. II Steph.*, pp. 150-151.
24. HG, p. 245.
25. *Ibid.*, pp. 246-247; *Ep. II Anselm.*, p. 158; Raim., p. 242.
26. HG, pp. 249, 256-257; Raim., pp. 243, 290; *Ep. II Anselm.*, p. 157; Rad., p. 647.

Christians were the autumn rains which drenched and chilled them, and which rusted their weapons and rotted their bow-strings; and upon the heels of the rains came the cold. [27] "This talk about the heat of Syria is all false," writes Stephen of Blois to his wife. "The winter here is just like our Western winter." [28]

The critical situation with regard to the food decided the crusading leaders to send an expedition in search of supplies to the hitherto un-ravaged Mohammedan country to the east. The plan may have originated in the mind of Bohemond; at all odds, he volunteered and was chosen to lead the expedition, in company with Robert of Flanders. A strong force, comprising both foot and horse, set out on December 28 for the district about Aleppo. For three days, Bohemond and Robert scoured the country, seizing what meagre supplies of food they found and on December 31 had the misfortune to encounter near el-Bara [29] a Turkish army made up of contingents from Jerusalem, Damascus, and Aleppo which was coming to the aid of Yagi Siyan.

The Turks divided their forces and attempted to surround the Franks, but the attacks of Robert and Bohemond soon routed them. The expedition continued its search for food to the north, [30] and returned to Antioch soon afterwards. Before returning to his camp, Bohemond explored the hilly region to the west of Antioch in search of food, but found that the wandering bands of pilgrims whom he encountered had stripped the country bare. Contenting himself with berating them for risking their lives in the Turk-infested country, he returned to his own camp, "victorious but empty-handed." [31]

The sufferings and privations of the besieging army, which had scarcely been alleviated by the results of Bohemond's foraging expedition, were not to be borne by some of the less enduring members of the army. Some of the poorer pilgrims, the insignificant folk who could not buy provisions, stole away into the mountains or to the sea-ports, [32] while even such prominent members of the host as William of Melun and Peter the Hermit won lasting obloquy by attempting flight, presumably with the intention of reaching the coast, and boarding a vessel for the west. They were pursued, however, and halted by

---

27. Rad., p. 647.
28. *Ep. II Steph.*, p. 150.
29. Kamal-ad-Din, pp. 578-579.
30. *Ibid.*
31. HG, pp. 249-253, 255-256; Alb., pp. 374-375; Raim., p. 244; *Ep. II Anselm.*, p. 158; *Ep. II Steph.*, p. 150.
32. HG, p. 265.

Tancred, who exacted from them the promise that they would return peaceably with him. On their return to the camp, William was conducted to Bohemond's quarters, where on the next day he was harshly upbraided by the Norman leader for his faithlessness and compelled to promise that he would not again attempt flight. [33]

The news of the mobilization of a Turkish expedition under Rudwan of Aleppo to raise the siege caused a fresh defection in the camp of the Crusaders, that of the imperial representative, Taticius. His part in the siege seems to have been an insignificant one, for he is seldom mentioned in the sources. According to Raymond of Agiles, he advised the leaders continually to leave the close vicinity of Antioch and take up their positions in the various neighbouring fortresses, whence they might maintain a loose blockade of the city. [34] Probably this advice was inspired by a desire to delay the progress of the siege until Alexius, who was busy reoccupying Asia Minor, could reach Antioch with a Greek army.

The author of the *Gesta Francorum* [35] and Albert of Aachen [36] agree that the news of the impending Turkish offensive caused his flight, although he attempted to conceal the fact by declaring that he was going to Asia Minor to arrange for the sending of food ships to relieve the distress of the Crusaders. He left behind him his camp and troops, no doubt few in number, as a pledge that he would return. [37] According to the account of Raymond of Agiles, Taticius circulated the lying rumour that Alexius was approaching with an army and hastened off as if to meet him, after handing over Tarsus, Mamistra, and Adana to Bohemond. [38] The three western sources, then, including Raymond, are unanimous in placing the responsibility for Taticius' departure upon the Greek representative himself, and in accusing him of faithlessness.

Anna Comnena, on the other hand, attempts to excuse the conduct of her father's official by throwing the blame for his departure upon Bohemond. According to her, Bohemond, who was already in communication with the Turkish officer who later betrayed the city to the Christians, was anxious to get rid of the Greek representative in order that nothing might thwart his own designs upon Antioch.

33. HG, pp. 258-260.
34. Raim., p. 245.
35. HG, pp. 261-262.
36. Alb., p. 417.
37. HG, pp. 261-264.
38. Raim., p. 246.

He therefore took Taticius aside, and informed him that the crusading leaders were convinced that the Turkish army under Kerboga of Mosul which was approaching had been summoned against them by Alexius, and that they had decided to take their revenge by killing Alexius' representative; Taticius must therefore look out for the safety of himself and his army. The famine and the desperate plight of the crusading army, however, seem to have been the deciding factors in his departure. Leaving the camp, he went to the Port of St. Simeon and thence on the Greek fleet to Cyprus. [39]

The determination of the truth as to Taticius' departure is a matter of some importance. If the *Gesta Francorum* and Raymond are correct, the Greeks were guilty of breaking their agreement with the Crusaders, for instead of aiding them at Antioch, the imperial legate had fled in cowardly fashion, leaving the Crusaders to their fate, and the *basileus* might justly be regarded as having forfeited some of his claims to Antioch. If, on the other hand, Anna is telling the truth, Taticius can hardly be blamed for his departure; the Greeks had, on the whole, lived up to the agreement made at Constantinople, and the whole episode is proof of the unscrupulousness of Bohemond and of his dishonest designs upon Antioch.

Chalandon, in accordance with his policy of defending Greek policy against the charges of the Crusaders, has chosen in his *Essai sur le règne d'Alexis 1er Comnène* to accept Anna's word and to lay the responsibility for Taticius' departure upon Bohemond. He finds in Raymond of Agiles evidence that the crusading leaders had already promised Antioch to Bohemond before the departure of Taticius, and he chooses to regard Raymond's statement that Taticius handed over a number of Cilician cities to Bohemond as the Provençal historian's version of a vague rumour of some sort of negotiation, which had taken place between Bohemond and Taticius.

> *Raimond ne sait pas bien ce dont Il s'agit, mais il a entendu dire que le général grec avait cédé à Bohémond deux ou trois villes. Cette façon même de dire deux ou trois villes montre qu'il n'est que l'écho de la rumeur publique et n'est par très certain de ce qu'il avance.*

Raymond then tends to confirm Anna. Bohemond, with the promise of Antioch in his wallet, undoubtedly got rid of Taticius in some such way as Anna charges. So far Chalandon. [40]

---

39. Anna, 2, pp. 86-87.
40. Chalandon, *Alexis*, pp. 201-202.

Let us examine the evidence more closely. The inaccuracies of Anna's account are obvious. In January, 1098, Bohemond was not yet in communication with Firuz, the future betrayer of Antioch, nor was it the approach of Kerboga but that of Rudwan of Aleppo which the Crusaders were preparing to meet at the time of Taticius' flight. [41] The errors are not calculated to increase our confidence in Anna's narrative.

Now, what truth is there in Chalandon's assumption that Bohemond had already in January, 1098, received the promise of Antioch from the crusading leaders? Raymond of Agiles, who is Chalandon's source for this statement, is undoubtedly specific in his assertion of the fact. According to him, Bohemond, evidently in January, 1098, threatened to leave the siege and return to Europe. His losses of men and horses had been grave and he was not rich enough, he said, to sustain the burden of such a prolonged siege. "We afterwards learned that he said this," writes Raymond, "because, overweeningly ambitious, he coveted the city of Antioch." As a result of the threat, however, the leaders, with the exception of Raymond of Toulouse, promised Bohemond Antioch, when it should be captured, and swore that they would not leave the siege, though it should last for seven years. [42]

Raymond's version, circumstantial as it is, is contradicted by the *Gesta Francorum*[43] Albert of Aachen, [44] and William of Tyre, who, in the portion of the narrative devoted to the capture of Antioch, has used a source unknown to us. [45] Bohemond did not make his bid for Antioch until May, when he had received Firuz's promise to betray the city, and it was not until the news of the approach of Kerboga's army that the crusading leaders agreed that the city should go to him if he succeeded in taking it. The chronological authority of the *Gesta*, composed as the book was, during the expedition itself, is undeniable, and receives conclusive confirmation from Albert and William.

Chalandon, however, who has not noticed the confirmation which Albert and William give to the *Gesta*, prefers Raymond's version to that of the *Gesta*, "*car il y a, dans la conduite de Bohémond, telle qu'il la rapporte, un côté assez peu glorieux, et il est tout naturel que l'auteur des Gesta*

41. Hagenmeyer has already noted these errors, HG, p. 263, n. 12.
42. Raim., pp. 245-246.
43. HG, pp. 296-298.
44. Alb., pp. 399-400.
45. WT, pp. 213-222. We learn from William that Raymond of Toulouse refused to be a party to the promise of Antioch to Bohemond, a fact upon which all the other sources, with the exception of Raymond of Agiles, are silent. WT, pp. 215, 220.

ait cherché à présenter les faits sous un jour plus avantageux pour le prince normand"; [46] in other words, the author of the *Gesta* has falsified his facts in order to defend Bohemond an entirely unjustifiable accusation, we believe. The author of the *Gesta* was a member of Bohemond's army and is undeniably anti-Greek, but there is no particle of evidence that he was in sympathy with Bohemond's territorial ambitions or has sought to justify his leader's tendency to elevate his own interests above those of the expedition as a whole.

On the contrary, pious Christian and faithful Crusader that he was, he reveals in that portion of his book which was written after the defeat of Kerboga [47] his displeasure at Bohemond's self-seeking policy, by omitting the laudatory epithets, with which in the earlier portions of his narrative he graces each mention of the name of his chief. It is not the author of the *Gesta* and Albert who are in error but Raymond.

The reason for his blunder is not difficult to discover. Raymond, unlike the author of the *Gesta*, did not compose his *Historia Francorum* until after the close of the Crusade. His memory in this case as in others has played him false. He associates quite correctly the promise of Antioch to Bohemond with the rumour of the approach of a Mohammedan army but he has made the episode precede the coming of Rudwan instead of that of Kerboga, a not unnatural mistake, very similar to Anna's error which we have already noted. Hence his error in placing the promise in January, instead of in May, 1098. [48]

There is little left, then, of Chalaadon's theory, for we have disposed of the motivation for Bohemond's effort to drive away Taticius early in 1098, when the suffering of the army before Antioch was at its height and every available man and horse was needed to aid in the siege, and when the hope of capturing the city was very dim.

But what of the negotiations between Bohemond and Taticius of which Chalandon finds a suggestion in Raymond's statement that the Greek general handed over two or three cities, Tarsus, Mamistra, and Adana, to Bohemond before he left the camp? One might ask why a vague rumour of negotiations between Bohemond and Taticius should be embodied by Raymond in precisely this form. Why the specific mention of the Cilician cities, if they did not have some connection with Taticius' departure?

---

46. Chalandon, *Alexis*, pp. 202-203.
47. This latter portion begins with ch. 30.
48. He has made another error in chronology in the same portion of the narrative, misdating the building of the fortress above Bohemond's camp. See HChr, no. 212.

Raymond's statement, we believe, is undeniably evidence of nego-
tiations between Bohemond and Taticius, but negotiations of a differ-
ent sort from those understood by Chalandon. In January, 1098, the
Cilician cities were already in Norman hands. Tancred had occupied
Mamistra and Adana in his campaign in Cilicia in September and
October, 1097, and Tarsus, which had been captured and garrisoned
by Baldwin, had probably also been taken over by the Normans. [49]
If there is no question, then, of Taticius' handing over these cities to
Bohemond in 1098, what have they to do with the Byzantine's departure? According to the *Gesta Francorum*, Taticius left behind him
his camp and attendants as a pledge that he would return. [50] Nothing
is more likely, I think, than that he allowed Bohemond, who already
held the Cilician cities, to retain them as an additional pledge of his
good faith and his intention to return to Antioch.

There is no evidence, then, of any weight, that Bohemond was
responsible for Taticius' departure, but, on the contrary, it would seem
that in accordance with his previous efforts to prevent the disper-
sion of the Christian forces, [51] he strove to guarantee Taticius' return.
Anna's account, its errors aside, is at best a childish story, and even she
seems to think that Taticius' despair of the success of the siege and the
hardships of the army were the real reasons for his flight. [52] Later, in
her own narrative, she inserts what purports to be a letter written by
Bohemond in answer to Alexius' demand of the surrender of Antioch,
in which the Norman claims that the flight of Taticius constituted a
violation of the agreement between the *basileus* and the Crusaders. [53]

Conceding, for the sake of argument, that Bohemond already
had designs upon Antioch, a theory for which there is no conclusive
evidence, one must still admit that there is no proof that it was his
machinations which drove Taticius from the siege in the dark days of
February.

The plan adopted for dealing with the threatening attack of Rudwan was originated by Bohemond himself. If the Franks waited until
the army from Aleppo reached Antioch, they would be caught between the Turks within the city and those under Rudwan. At a meeting held in the quarters of Adhemar, the papal legate, it was decided

49. See *supra*, chapter 4.
50. HG, p. 263.
51. See *supra*, chapter 4.
52. Anna, 2, p. 87.
53. Anna, 2, p. 112.

therefore, on Bohemond's advice, to march out to meet Rudwan's army instead of awaiting it in camp; the foot-soldiers were to be left behind and the army was to be composed solely of horsemen. [54] Since many of the horses had died during the march through Asia Minor and Armenia or in the course of the siege, the Crusaders could muster only seven hundred horsemen. [55] The little army, accompanied by a few foot-soldiers, set out on the evening of February 8, and camped for the night between the Orontes and the Lake of Antioch.

In the morning, Bohemond's scouts reported that the enemy, who had spent the night near Harem, was approaching in two columns. Bohemond, who appears to have been appointed commander-in-chief shortly before the opening of the engagement, an event which throws some light upon the impromptu method of righting a battle in the eleventh century, drew up the army in five divisions under as many leaders on a narrow strip of land between the river and the lake, while he himself commanded a sixth division, which was stationed in the rear as a reserve. [56] The Turks began the battle with a shower of arrows, followed by a cavalry attack, which forced the Franks to give ground. The charge, however, of the reserve division under Bohemond's constable, Robert, and Bohemond himself, turned the tide of battle and the Turks were put to flight and pursued as far as the Iron Bridge. The Franks captured a considerable amount of spoil, including a number of horses, and the fortress of Harem as well. [57]

The Crusaders, now that the dangers of an attempt to raise the siege were temporarily removed, once more directed their attention to Antioch. In March the army undertook to draw more closely the siege lines around the city, an effort in which Bohemond and his Normans played an important part. As early as November, 1097, the Franks had constructed a fortress on the summit of Maregart, a hill overlooking Bohemond's camp, [58] and on March 5, it was decided to build a fortress in the Mohammedan cemetery near the Bridge Gate, in order to prevent all further egress from the northern side of the city. [59] On the same day, Bohemond and Raymond of Toulouse set out for the Port of St. Simeon in order to bring back workmen, tools,

---

54. HG, pp. 265-267; Raim., p. 246.
55. HG, p. 247; *Ep. II Steph.,* p. 151; *Ep. II Anselm.,* p. 158.
56. HG, pp. 268-269; Raim., p. 247.
57. Raim., p. 247; HG, pp. 270-275; *Ep. II Steph.,* p. 150; *Ep. II Anselm.,* p. 158.
58. HG, p. 248; *Ep. II Anselm.,* p. 157.
59. *Epistula cleri et populi Luccensis ad omnes fideles,* in HEp, p. 166.

and building materials from the Genoese and English ships in the harbour. On returning later in the week, the expedition was suddenly attacked by an army of Turks from Antioch. Bohemond, deserted by his followers, escaped capture only through the bravery of a certain Reginald Porchet, who himself was taken prisoner by the Turks. Having returned with a small number of their men, Bohemond and Raymond were joined by an army from the camp, and, fiercely attacking the Turks who had begun to re-enter the city, killed a great number of them outright and drove many others into the river. [60]

The fortress before the Bridge Gate was handed over, on its completion, to Raymond of Toulouse to guard, and proved most effective in preventing further successful raids on the Christian camp from that direction, [61] while the city was still more narrowly invested when Tancred was sent to fortify the Monastery of St. George to the west of the city, near the gate of that name. [62] All of the five principal gates of the city were now blockaded by the Franks.

The situation of the Turks within Antioch had now become serious, if not critical. The question of provisioning the city must have been a serious one even before its complete investment; now there remained only the postern gates opening on the hills through which provisions could be introduced, and the energetic Tancred did much to make these entrances of little use to the Turks. [63] Only the arrival of Mohammedan reinforcements could save the city from falling eventually into the hands of the Crusaders. But let the Turks hold out for a few months longer and Yagi Siyan would receive an answer to his frantic summons for aid in the shape of a great army under Kerboga of Mosul which was even then on its way toward Antioch. A large part of the population, however, had grown weary of the siege, and the perils of hunger and the exactions of Yagi Siyan had made many, Mohammedan and Christian alike, indifferent to the fate of the city. Among this number was Firuz, a Turk or renegade Armenian, [64] who

---

60. HG, pp. 280-284; *Hist. bel. sacr.*, pp. 191-192; Raim., pp. 248-249; *Ep. II Steph.*, pp. 151-152; Cafarus, *De liberatione civitatum Orientis*, in *Rec., Hist, occ.*, 5, p. 50.
61. *Ep. II Anselm.*, p. 158; HG, p. 287.
62. HG, pp. 289-291; Raim., p. 250.
63. HG, pp. 291-292.
64. The sources disagree as to the nationality of Firuz. Bohemond's own letter, the *Gesta*, Kamal-ad-Dîn, and Fulk of Chartres make him a Turk, while Anna Comnena and Ralph of Caen declare he was an Armenian. *Epistula Boemundi . . . ad Urbanum II papam*, in HEp, p. 162; HG, p. 293; Kamal-ad-Dîn, p. 580; HF, p. 231; Anna, 2, p. 86; Rad., p. 651; WT, p. 212.

commanded one or more towers on the western wall of the city. With a view to betraying the city into the hands of the Crusaders, he had opened negotiations with Bohemond, whom he seems to have regarded as the leader of the Christian army, because of the latter's activity in the conduct of the siege and the fame of his campaigns against Alexius which had spread to the East. [65]

We do not know how or exactly when the negotiations were begun. Bohemond plied him with messages, urging him to promise to betray the city to him whenever he should demand it, and pledging him a liberal reward for his part in the affair. Firuz finally consented, and fortified with his promise, the Norman approached the other leaders in May and made his first bid for Antioch. Here at last we are on safe ground and see Bohemond set upon the acquisition of the city for himself. His proposal was a veiled one, for instead of demanding the city outright, he suggested that they agree that it be granted to the man who should succeed in taking it. The plan was voted down, however, with the argument that since all had shared in the labour of the siege, so all should partake of the benefits of its capture. [66]

News, however, of the approach of Kerboga's army which reached the Christian camp not long afterward, changed the situation materially. The Crusaders could not hope to defeat Kerboga as they had Rudwan and disaster seemed to be threatening. Taking stock of their desperate situation, the council of the leaders was forced to reverse its recent decision, and promise the city to Bohemond. It is important to note that though in desperate straits, the leaders remembered their oath to Alexius, and promised Bohemond that if he succeeded in capturing Antioch he might keep it, only on the condition that if the *basileus* came to their aid and adhered to his other promises, the Norman was to turn over the city to him; if Alexius failed them, Bohemond might retain Antioch as his own possession. [67] Only Raymond of Toulouse refused his assent to the agreement. [68] He too had designs upon Antioch, and we shall see how the rivalry between Norman and Provençal becomes more and more bitter as time passes.

Having obtained the desired promise, Bohemond communicated with Firuz, informing him that the time had come for the betrayal of

---

65. Rad., p. 652; Alb., pp. 344-345. Ibn el-Athîr likewise regards Bohemond as the commander-in-chief of the Christian army. Ibn el-Athîr, p. 194.
66. HG, pp. 293-297.
67. HG, pp. 297-298; Rad., pp. 653-654; Alb., p. 400; Anna, 2, pp. 89; Raim., p. 246.
68. *Ibid.*; WT, pp. 212-214.

the city. The Oriental answered on June 1 that he was ready to keep his word, sent his son as a hostage, and suggested that on the following evening, the Franks pretend to start out as if for an expedition into the Saracen country to the east in order to allay the suspicions of the garrison, and then encircle the city in the dark, and appear before that section of the wall which he guarded. Bohemond adopted the proposal, gave orders on June 2 for the mobilization of a body of troops, ostensibly for a raid into Turkish territory that night, and only then ommunicated the plan of action to Godfrey of Bouillon, Robert of Flanders, Raymond of Toulouse, and Adhemar of Puy. [69]

The expedition under Bohemond, who was accompanied by Godfrey and Robert of Flanders,[70] left the camp early in the evening. Marching east and south at first, it gradually changed its direction, and encircling the city through the hills arrived shortly before daybreak at Firuz's tower, the Tower of the Two Sisters, which was situated not far from the Gate of St. George. [71] A messenger from Firuz warned the Franks to wait until the patrol which was making its round of the walls should pass. [72] After the guard with its flaring torches had made its way through the Tower of the Two Sisters and had passed on, the Crusaders approached the tower and began to mount the rope-ladder which had been fastened to the battlements. About sixty Franks gained the walls and occupied three of the towers. Firuz was alarmed at the small number of the invaders, and inquired for Bohemond, who was soon summoned from below by an Italian sergeant. The Crusaders on the walls spread along the curtain, seizing other towers and killing their garrisons, as they raised their battle-cry, "*Deus le volt*," which was taken up by those below. [73]

For a short time, the success of the whole attack seemed to hang in the balance, for the rope-ladder, overtaxed by the weight of the men who were struggling upwards to the battlements, suddenly gave way, pitching those who were on it to the ground, and cutting off communication with the Franks who were fighting desperately on the walls. The Crusaders below, however, soon discovered a postern gate near the tower, broke it in, and rushed into the city. All Antioch was now in an uproar, and just as the day was dawning, the Christians in

69. HG, pp. 298-300.
70. Raim., p. 251; Alb., p. 400.
71. WT, p. 212. See Rey, *Étude sur les monuments*, pp. 196 ff.
72. Raim., p. 251.
73. HG, pp. 302-304; Alb., pp. 402-403; HF, pp. 232-233.

the camp on the Orontes, aroused by the shouts and screams, beheld the red banner of Bohemond waving over the city on the hill near the citadel where he had planted it. [74] Rushing to the walls, they entered through the gates which had been opened by their comrades within the city. [75]

Then followed all the horrors of a medieval sack. The Turks seem to have offered little resistance, and those who were fortunate enough to escape the swords of the Christians fled out of the city, or took refuge in the citadel above the town. Bohemond, realizing the importance of the citadel, attacked it fiercely but, wounded in the thigh, he was compelled to give up the attempt. [76] In the meanwhile, Yagi Siyan, who had fled from the city, had been captured by a number of Armenian peasants, who brought the head, baldric and sheath of the murdered *emir* to Bohemond in the hope of receiving a reward. Antioch fell on June 3, 1098. [77]

The Crusaders had taken the city only just in time, for on the day following the advance-guard of Kerboga's army appeared before the walls, and the attack on the citadel, which the Franks had planned, was postponed. [78] On the eighth, Kerboga began the siege in earnest, and leading a division of his army to the south of the city, introduced a portion of his troops into the citadel under the command of Achmed ibn Merwan. [79]

The lot of the Christians was now a serious one, attacked from without by the greater part of Kerboga's army, and continually menaced from within by the garrison of the citadel. Despairing of the fate of the expedition, on the night of the tenth, Bohemond's brother-in-law, William of Grantmesnil, and other knights let themselves down from the walls by means of ropes, and fled away to the Port of St. Simeon, while only the activity of Bohemond and the Bishop of Puy prevented the escape of others. [80] Soon after this episode, each of the leaders took an oath that he would not flee. The oath was prob-

---

74. HG, pp. 305-307; Raim., p. 251; HF, p. 234; Alb., p. 404. Bohemond's banner is reputed to have borne the representation of a serpent. *Fragment d'une chanson d'Antioche en provençal*, in *Archives de l'Orient latin*, 2, Documents, p. 485.

75. HG, p. 307; Rad., p. 655.

76. Rob. Mon., pp. 806-807; Gilo, *Historia de via Hierosolymitana*, in *Rec., Hist, occ.*, 5, pp. 767-768; *Ep. Boemundi ad Urbanum II*, p. 162.

77. HG, p. 310; Raim., p. 252; Rad., p. 655; Alb., pp. 406-407; *Ep. II Anselm.*, p. 159.

78. HF, p. 242; *Ep. Boemundi ad Urbanum II* p. 162.

79. *Ibid.*, Raim., p. 253; HG, p. 330; Kamal-ad-Din, p. 582.

80. HG, pp. 33 2 -335; Raim., p. 253; Alb., pp. 414-415; Anna, 2, p. 96.

ably proposed by Bohemond, for he is said to have been the first to swear.[81]

Throughout the rest of the campaign about Antioch, Bohemond continues to be the principal and dominating figure in the crusading army. He was indefatigable in his efforts to guard the city, spending his days in directing the operations against the citadel and a part of his nights in making the rounds of the walls, watching over the safety of the city and seeking to prevent further desertions.[82] About the twentieth of June, he was chosen to act as *generalissimo* of the army until two weeks after the completion of the campaign against Kerboga.[83]

The Norman's immediate task was the siege of the citadel and the guarding of the valley which led down into the city, and fierce and frequent fighting took place between the Turks and Bohemond's Normans who held the towers and walls adjacent to the fortress.[84] One of his chief difficulties in the operations was the lack of troops. Many of the Franks, either through sloth or fear, had hidden themselves in the houses throughout the city. The task of searching them out was a hopeless one, and Bohemond took the drastic steps of ordering the quarter of the city about the palace of Yagi Siyan to be set on fire, in order to drive out the slackers from their hiding-places. He effected his end, but a brisk wind spread the flames, which for a time became uncontrollable. The fire was extinguished by midnight, after having destroyed about two thousand buildings.[85]

Realizing the inadequacy of the Christian defences against the garrison in the citadel, Bohemond and Raymond constructed a strong wall across the valley between the two hills and a fortress equipped with hurling machines for use against the enemy within the city.[86] Albert of Aachen chronicles a Turkish attack on the new fortifications, which would have resulted disastrously for Bohemond's forces, had it not been for the aid of Godfrey and the two Roberts.[87]

The Christians, weak and dispirited from lack of food and the almost incessant attacks of the enemy, waited in vain for the appearance of Alexius and the imperial army. The *basileus*, after reconquering the important cities on the western coast of Asia Minor, had marched

---

81. HG, p. 340. Cf. Raim., p. 253; Alb., pp. 414-415; Anna, 2, p. 96.
82. Baldr. Dol., p. 65, variation 4; WT, p. 243.
83. Raim., p. 258; HChr, no. 286.
84. HG, pp. 345-346; 349-350.
85. HG, pp. 347-349; Rad., pp. 660-661.
86. HG, p. 349; Raim., p. 253; Alb., p. 409; Rad., pp. 659-660.
87. Alb., p. 410.

south in the company of Guy, the half-brother of Bohemond, and a considerable force of Franks, with the intention of joining the Crusaders at Antioch, and thus fulfilling his agreement. He was met at Philomelium by Stephen of Blois, who had left the army for Alexandretta shortly before the capture of Antioch and had fled thence after the arrival of Kerboga, and by William of Grantmesnil and the other "rope-walkers" from Antioch. [88]

They brought him the news of the terrible plight of the Crusaders in Antioch, assuring him that their annihilation was certain, and advising him to return to Constantinople. This intelligence and the news that a Saracen army under Ismael, the son of the sultan of Bagdad, was even then approaching persuaded Alexius, in spite of the protests of Guy to give up his plans of cooperating with the Franks; so, giving orders to devastate the country in order to check the advance of the enemy, he and his army returned to Constantinople. [89] The Crusaders were again to discover on how weak a reed they leaned, when they relied upon the promises of Greek aid.

The waning hopes of the Christians in Antioch were revived on June 14 by what was regarded as a new manifestation of God's favour toward them. A Provençal peasant in the army of Raymond of Toulouse, Peter Bartholomew by name, appeared before the count and Adhemar of Puy on June 10, with the story that St. Andrew had appeared to him five times, and had directed him to inform Raymond that the lance which had pierced the side of Christ on the cross was buried in the Church of St. Peter in Antioch, and that if it was recovered, it would bring victory to the Crusaders. In spite of Adhemar's scepticism, Raymond seems to have believed the man's story; digging with other Provençal Crusaders in the designated place on June 14, the day appointed by St. Andrew in the vision, Peter Bartholomew produced a lance which the common people believed to be and which Raymond accepted as the Holy Lance. [90]

It is impossible to discover the attitude of the other leaders or to ascertain whether the Normans already displayed towards the lance the scepticism which they were afterward to affect, but it is very probably that they viewed askance the production of a relic of doubtful authenticity, which only served to enhance the reputation and prestige

88. HG, pp. 353-354; Raim., p. 258; HF, p. 228.
89. HG, pp. 355-362; Anna, 2, pp. 96-99; Rad., pp. 658-659; Alb., pp. 417-418.
90. Raim., pp. 253-255; 257-258; HG, pp. 341-345 ', 362-363; Rad., pp. 676-677; *Ep. II Anselm.*, p. 159; HF, pp. 235-237.

of Raymond of Toulouse. [91] We may be fairly sure that the guardianship of the lance did not serve to elevate Raymond in the estimation of the important crusading chiefs, since it is Bohemond and not he who is chosen to act as *generalissimo* of the army.

The crusading chiefs, either because they believed that Christ had manifested himself in the discovery of the lance, or more likely because they saw that the belief of the army in the relic had stirred up the host to a wild enthusiasm which would be most efficacious in the battle with the Turks, seemed to be encouraged by the finding of the weapon and decided to risk a pitched battle with Kerboga. [92] Therefore a three-days' fast was declared, and on June 27, Peter the Hermit and Herluin were sent as ambassadors to Kerboga to offer peace terms, which the Turks seem to have straightway rejected. [93]

On the next day, June 28, 1098, the Christian forces pre pared for battle. The army, under the command of Bohemond, was divided into four great double divisions, the first consisting of the French and Normans under the command of Hugh of Vermandois and the two Roberts, the second of the Burgundians and Lotharingians under Godfrey of Bouillon, the third of the *Provençals* under Adhemar of Puy, for Raymond was ill and had been left behind to mask the citadel, and the fourth of the Normans of southern Italy under the command of Bohemond himself. [94]

The army, consisting of both horse and foot, marched out of the city through the Bridge Gate, and deployed in excellent order into the plain beyond, forming a line whose right wing under Hugh and the Roberts rested on the Orontes and whose left under Adhemar on the mountains some two thousand paces to the north. Bohemond, who commanded the largest division, held his troops behind the line as a reserve, in accordance with his usual custom.

A Turkish attempt to flank the Christian left wing was successfully thwarted, and the burning of the grass on the plain by the Turks proved no more efficacious in checking the Christian attack. Unable to withstand any longer the pressure of the Frankish soldiery, Kerboga's line broke and fled, hotly pursued by Tancred and the Christian cavalry. The victory was complete, the siege was raised, and Antioch and the crusading army were now safe from the immediate attack of

91. Rad., p. 677. See Kugler, *Albert*, pp. 146-147.

92. HG, p. 363.

93. *Ibid.*, pp. 363-368; Raim., p. 259; HF, pp. 247-250; *Ep. II Anselm.*, p. 160.

94. Raim., p. 259; HF, p. 255. Cf. HG, pp. 368-371.

the Mohammedans of northern Syria. [95]

The commander of the Turkish garrison in the citadel, Achmed ibn Merwan, beholding the defeat of his compatriots, surrendered on the same day. He at first accepted unwittingly Raymond's standard, which he raised above the citadel, but learning the identity of its owner from some Italian soldiers, he later replaced it with the banner of Bohemond, the real commander of the expedition. The Norman granted the garrison, which numbered a thousand men, the option of remaining and becoming Christians or of receiving a safe-conduct to their own country. The *emir* and some of his men accepted Christianity and were baptized. [96]

Although the city had been captured through Bohemond's diplomacy and Kerboga defeated largely by his leadership, Antioch was not yet his either in title or in fact. There is no better proof of the good faith of the crusading leaders as a whole and their desire to fulfil the terms of their oath to Alexius than their decision soon after the defeat of Kerboga to send legates to the *basileus* offering him the city. It is possible, of course, that the Crusaders did not yet know that Alexius had fled from Philomelium and deserted them in their hour of need,[97] and yet they realized that they had looked in vain for Greek aid while they lay starving before Antioch and afterward when it seemed that the expedition would be destroyed by Kerboga. Alexius had not carried out his share of the bargain, and if the leaders had respected their promise to Bohemond, they would have surrendered the city to him. Instead they sent Hugh of Vermandois and Baldwin of Hainault to Constantinople, informing Alexius of the defeat of Kerboga and requesting him to come to receive Antioch, and fulfil the promise of personal participation in the war with the Turks which he had made to them. [98] One may well doubt whether Bohemond was a willing party to the sending of the legates, for the act was an open violation of the leaders' promise to him.

Even at this date, the chief obstacle in the council of the leaders to the realization of Bohemond's ambitions must have been found

---

95. HG, pp. 368-379; Raim., pp. 259-261; *Ep. II Anselm.*, p. 160; *Ep. Boemundi ad Urbanum, II*, p. 163; HF, pp. 255-257; Alb., pp. 421-427; Rad., pp. 666-672.

96. HG, pp. 379-381; *Ep. Boemundi ad Urbanum II*, p. 164; Alb., p. 434. Cf. Raim., pp. 261-262.

97. According to one manuscript of Baldric of Dol, two of Bohemond's friends with Guy's army succeeded in reaching Antioch with the news of Alexius' retreat. Baldr. Dol., p. 73, n. 17.

98. HG, pp. 382-383; HF, p. 258; Alb., pp. 434-435; Gislebert, p. 504.

in the stubborn opposition of Raymond of Toulouse. The ill-feeling between the two princes had undoubtedly begun at Constantinople when Bohemond forced Raymond to make a partial submission to Alexius, and the breach between Norman and Provençal had been widened by clashes between their foraging parties during the siege of Antioch,[99] and later on by the sceptical and mocking attitude of the Normans toward the Holy Lance. [100]

Most important of all, Raymond was a rival claimant to Antioch. True, he had no better grounds for his claim than his participation in the siege, grounds which all the other leaders might have urged with equal justice, but he had not been a party to the leaders' promise of Antioch to Bohemond, and he now refused to give up those portions of the city which he held. His men had been forcibly expelled from the citadel by the Normans, but *semper insatiatus desiderio acquirendi*, in the words of Albert of Aachen, he continued to hold and refused to surrender to Bohemond the Tower of the Bridge Gate and the Palace of Yagi Siyan. [101]

Although Antioch had not yet been formally granted to Bohemond, he acted as if it were already his, and on July 14, granted to the Genoese tax-free the Church of St. John, with a warehouse, a well, and thirty houses, and exempted them from all tolls and taxes in Antioch and its dependencies. [102] The Genoese, on their side, engaged themselves to aid in the defence of the city against all enemies, except the *Provençals*. In case Bohemond and Raymond were to take up arms, the Genoese were to attempt to reconcile them, and if unsuccessful, were to remain neutral. [103]

The quarrel between Bohemond and Raymond dragged on and finally threatened to disrupt the whole expedition. On August 1, Adhemar of Puy, the only person in the army who might possibly have brought about peace between the warring factions, died of the plague.[104] The princes, however, were still capable of enough cooperation to send a joint letter to the pope on the eleventh of September, a letter which was signed by Bohemond, Raymond, Godfrey, Robert of Normandy, Robert of Flanders, and Eustace. The influence of Ray-

---

99. Rad., p. 676.
100. *Ibid.*, pp. 678-679.
101. Raim., p. 262; HG, p. 397; Alb., p. 434.
102. HCh, no. 300.
103. *Pactum Genuensium*, in HEp, p. 156.
104. HG, p. 390; Raim., p. 262.

mond and his friends in the composition of the letter is perceptible in a mention of the Holy Lance, but the fact that Bohemond's name stands first in the enumeration of the princes in the salutation and that he occasionally uses the first person in the letter is evidence of his own commanding position in the army. [105]

A little later, several of the leaders left Antioch, Godfrey to go into the Edessan country, and Bohemond to Cilicia. [106] According to Albert, Bohemond joined Godfrey in an expedition against the Turks who were besieging Ezaz, but the other sources are silent on the subject. We know next to nothing of Bohemond's activities in Cilicia. He probably busied himself with the organization of Tancred's conquests, for William of Tyre mentions his presence in Tarsus, Adana, Mamistra and Ainzarba. [107]

On November 1 the leaders, according to their agreement, assembled at Antioch. Bohemond, who had been taken ill while sojourning in Cilicia, was somewhat late in arriving. [108] The question of the disposition of Antioch was no nearer settlement than it had ever been. It still divided the council of the princes and remained as the only obstacle in the way of the advance on Jerusalem. Bohemond continued daily to importune the leaders to hand over the whole city to him, according to the promise they had made to him before its capture, but Raymond stubbornly refused to give up the towers which he held.

The council of the leaders, which met in the Church of St. Peter, was so sharply divided by the question, that frequently there was danger that the debates would end in open battle. One party, composed in large part of Normans and of those who already held fortresses and towns in the vicinity of Antioch, argued that Antioch should be awarded to Bohemond since Alexius had not kept his agreement and had no intention of doing so, and that it would be folly to allow the city to fall once more into the hands of the Turks, instead of granting it to Bohemond, who enjoyed a great reputation among the Mohammedans. The *Provençals*, on the other hand, protested that they had sworn to Alexius that they would not retain any of his possessions except with his consent, and Raymond pointed out that he himself had taken the oath to Alexius at Bohemond's own solicitation. It is not to be assumed that Raymond was working in behalf of Alexius. His

105. *Ep. Boemundi ad Urbanum II*, pp. 161-165.
106. Alb., pp. 438-439.
107. WT, pp. 279-280.
108. Tudebod., p. 87.

single purpose was to keep Antioch from falling into the hands of his Norman rival, and his only effective argument against such a disposition of the city was to put forward the obligations which he and the other chiefs had assumed toward Alexius. [109]

There is reason to suppose that a majority of the leaders favoured Bohemond's claims. The Norman seems to have been on the best of terms with Godfrey, Robert of Normandy, and Robert of Flanders throughout the whole expedition, [110] while the greedy and irascible Provencal had few friends outside of his own army. Godfrey and Robert of Flanders were not averse to awarding the city to Bohemond, but feared to suggest it openly, lest they should be accused of perjury. [111] Most of the important leaders, in fact, in spite of their approval of Bohemond's position, remained noncommittal. [112]

The murmurs of the rank and file of the army, who objected to the delay in the advance on Jerusalem, caused by the wrangling of their chiefs, forced Raymond to propose a truce, a *pax discors* his chronicler calls it. The question of the disposition of the city was to be left in abeyance, both leaders were to accompany the expedition to Jerusalem, and Raymond promised to abide by whatever decision in the matter the leaders arrived at later, saving only his oath to the *basileus*. Bohemond accepted his rival's proposal, much against his will, no doubt, and obviously forced to do so by the sentiment of the crusading army in general. The agreement was sealed by the oaths of Norman and *Provençal*. The armed truce, however, in no way decreased the mutual suspicion of the rivals, for Bohemond strengthened and regarrisoned the citadel and Raymond fortified the Tower of the Bridge Gate and the Palace of Yagi Siyan with men and food. The city during the course of the expedition against Jerusalem would thus remain divided between the Norman and *Provençal* forces. [113]

On November 23 Raymond and Robert of Flanders left Antioch, presumably beginning the march on Jerusalem. On November 27 they arrived at Marra, the Maarat en-Numan of the Mohammedans, which they besieged on the next day. The same day saw the arrival of Bohemond. [114] The city was captured on December 11, and on that day, Bohemond promised the leading men of the town that if they and

109. Raim., p. 267; HG, pp. 394-395.
110. Cf. Alb., p. 295.
111. Raim., p. 267.
112. HG, p. 395.
113. Raim., pp. 267-268; HG, pp. 395-397.
114. HG, pp. 401-402; Raim., p. 268; Tudebod., p. 90.

their wives and children were to assemble in a designated spot near the gate he would save their lives. On the next day, however, when the city was given over to the army to sack, Bohemond despoiled his miserable prisoners of their goods, killed a number of them, and sent the rest to Antioch to be sold into slavery. [115]

The old trouble between Bohemond and Raymond now flamed up anew, when the former refused to hand over certain towers in Marra which he had seized, unless Raymond promised to cede the positions which he still held in Antioch. The fact that the Normans, who had played a minor part in the capture of the city, had taken a large part of the spoil, and that Bohemond and his men made sport of the revelations of Peter Bartholomew, the discoverer of the Holy Lance and *protégé* of Raymond, made the count doubly furious, but nothing would induce Bohemond to give up the towers. [116]

The people of the host, oppressed by famine and weary of the struggle of their leaders, were angered by this new delay in the advance on Jerusalem, and Bohemond's suggestion to postpone the departure until Easter was rejected. Raymond, because of his possession of the Lance, was finally acclaimed by the host as chief to lead it on to Jerusalem, much to the disgust of Bohemond, who left Marra for Antioch some four or five days later. [117] Without doubt, Bohemond's participation in the expedition against Marra had been caused by a desire to prevent the gain by Raymond of any strong or valuable positions in the region which he had decided was to be his own.

Raymond, however, was not to leave northern Syria without another attempt to adjust matters with Bohemond, and sent messengers to Godfrey, Robert of Flanders, Robert of Normandy, and Bohemond, asking them to come to confer with him at Rugia, the er-Ruj of the Turks. The conference, which was duly held, came to naught, for the leaders were unwilling to attempt to make peace between Bohemond and Raymond, unless the latter gave up the positions which he still held in Antioch. This Raymond obstinately refused to do, and Bohemond and the other leaders returned to Antioch, while Raymond rejoined his troops at Marra. [118]

On learning that the count had gone south from Marra, Bohe-

115. HG, pp. 407-409.
116. Raim., p. 270; Rad., p. 678.
117. Raim., pp. 270-271.
118. HG, pp. 411-412; Raim., p. 271. Robert the Monk mentions a subsequent meeting of the leaders at Kafr tab. Rob. Mon., p. 850.

mond ejected the *Provençal* troops by force from their towers in Antioch, and now remained as absolute master of the city. [119] According to Bartolf of Nangeio, the city was granted to Bohemond by common agreement, [120] but it is likely that the grant took the shape of a tacit recognition of a *fait accompli*.

On February 2, according to Albert of Aachen, the leaders who had been wintering with Bohemond at Antioch, including Godfrey and Robert of Flanders, decided to meet at Laodicea on March 1 to continue the advance toward Jerusalem. [121] They met as agreed upon, and started south to besiege Jabala, but Bohemond, instead of continuing with the expedition, returned to Antioch, thus violating the promise which he had made to Raymond in November. [122] The Norman was not to be a party to the capture of Jerusalem.

Sometime after the departure of the leaders, envoys of Alexius arrived at Antioch with an answer to the message which the Crusaders had sent to Constantinople with Hugh of Vermandois. Finding Bohemond in possession of the city, they demanded that he restore it to their master in accordance with the oath which he had taken at Constantinople, but the Norman refused, giving them a letter for Alexius, in which he accused the Greeks of having broken the agreement, first, because Taticius had deserted the army in the hour of need, and second, because Alexius had not come with an army as he had promised. Did the *basileus* think that it was just that he (Bohemond) should give up what he had obtained with so much labour and suffering? [123]

The Greek legates, instead of returning home, followed after the

---

119. Raim., p. 286; Rad., p. 675; Alb., p. 448; Tudebod., p. 95.

120. Bartolfus de Nangeio, p. 506.

121. Alb., p. 450.

122. Alb., p. 453; HG, pp. 428–429.

123. Anna, 2, pp. 111–113. The chronology of this portion of Anna's narrative, as is not unusual, is extremely involved. From her account, she would seem to place the sending of the legates to Bohemond in 1103–1104, for she dates it with reference to Tancred's capture of Laodicea. I hold with Kugler and against Chalandon that the Byzantine princess is in error. Anna was not very well informed as to events at Antioch, and indeed does not seem to have known that Tancred ever went to Jerusalem, and was called to Antioch only after Bohemond's capture by the Turks. In my opinion, she has confused the news of the capture of Laodicea with that of the capture of Antioch. The Greek demand for the return of Antioch, while natural enough early in 1099, shortly after Alexius had learned that Bohemond had laid claim to the city, is meaningless if placed in 1103, after Bohemond had been in possession of the city for four years. See Kugler, *Boemund und Tankred*, pp. 9–10, 59–60; Chalandon, *Alexis*, pp. 222, 234.

crusading army and came upon it at Arka early in April. They complained to the leaders of Bohemond's violation of his oath, and asked that the Crusaders delay their march to await the *basileus* who would arrive by St. John's Day. One party of the Franks, including Raymond of Toulouse, was for waiting for Alexius, but a larger group argued that the *basileus* had already displayed his treachery and faithlessness and that little was to be expected from his aid, and advised an immediate march on Jerusalem. Their counsel was adopted and the request of the Byzantine legates rejected. [124]

The Greek legates likewise demanded of Raymond the return of certain towns which he held. Anna, in her account which is involved as to its chronology, mentions Laodicea, Maraclea and Valania. [125] The history of Laodicea during the siege of Antioch is very difficult to educe from the mutually contradictory sources and need not concern us here. Suffice it to say, that there is evidence that Raymond's men in the spring of 1099 probably held the important seaport. [126] Valania had been captured by the

Franks during the siege of Antioch, [127] while Maraclea was taken by the *Provençals* in February, 1099. [128] Anna is of the opinion that her father made the demand for the return of the towns in writing. Basing his theory on this point, Chalandon has imagined that if Alexius was on such terms with Raymond of Toulouse in the early months of 1099 that he could personally demand of him the return of the former Byzantine possessions there must have been some earlier change in their relations and a *rapprochement* which took place probably in the summer of 1098, a *rapprochement* of which there is evidence in the policy of Raymond during his negotiations in November, 1098. [129]

I believe that Chalandon is in error. There is no evidence in Raymond's actions in November, 1098, that he was working for Alexius' and not for his own interests. As for the Greek demand for the return of the towns, it is much simpler to assume that Anna was mistaken, that there was no letter written by her father to Raymond, but that the Greek legates on learning that the count was occupying Laodicea, Maraclea and Valania, simply demanded these places of him in their master's name, just as they demanded from Bohemond the return of

124. Raim., p. 286.
125 Anna, 2, p. 105.
126 Alb., p. 501.
127. Rad., p. 650.
128. HG, p. 428.
129. Chalandon, *Alexis*, pp. 212-213.

Antioch. In April, 1099, Raymond realized that his chances of obtaining Antioch had disappeared, for Bohemond was then in complete control of the city. He therefore decided to throw in his lot with Alexius against their common enemy, Bohemond, and handed over to the Greek legates the towns which they demanded. It was to be expected, under these circumstances, that he would support, as he did, Alexius' request that the Crusaders await his coming. The *rapprochement* between Raymond and the Greeks, then, dates from April, 1099.

It will be not unprofitable to review briefly the circumstances which made possible the retention by Bohemond of Antioch. The older historians of the First Crusade, who followed faithfully and somewhat uncritically their Western sources, were general in their opinion that the Greeks had been to blame for all the difficulties which arose between them and the Crusaders, that Alexius was little better than a traitor and was personally responsible for most of the disasters suffered by the Franks. Later scholars have adopted a more critical attitude and have shown that by no means entire justice has been done to the Greek side of the question. Among these scholars is Chalandon, whose valuable work we have so often had occasion to mention.

Chalandon finds in Bohemond the real villain of the piece. He agrees with the theory that the Crusades were a baneful series of events for the Byzantine Empire, [130] he remarks sympathetically that "the Greeks regarded the Crusaders as invaders more civilized, but so much the more dangerous, than the Petchenegs and the Polovtzes," [131] and he attempts to show that the Crusaders were really the mercenaries of Alexius. [132] According to Chalandon, Alexius fulfilled faithfully all of his engagements toward the Crusaders; Taticius did not flee but was driven from Antioch by Bohemond's ruse; [133] Alexius intended to join the Franks before Antioch, and the fault for his failure to do so was not his own but that of Stephen of Blois and his fellow fugitives. [134] Bohemond with his perfidious designs on Antioch was responsible for the first breach in the agreement, [135] and the other leaders by their refusal in April, 1099, to await the coming of the *basileus* were guilty of an act of bad faith towards Alexius, who had thus far remained loyal

130. Chalandon. *Alexis*, p. 159.
131. *Ibid.*, p. 160.
132. *Ibid.*, pp. 164–165, 191.
133. *Ibid.*, pp. 200–203.
134. *Ibid.*, pp. 203–205.
135. Ibid., pp. 205-206.

in word and deed to the Crusaders. [136]

As an account of the Greek position, Chalandon's version is valuable; as a perfectly accurate history, it stands in need of qualification and correction.

That the Crusades as a whole were harmful to the welfare of the Byzantine Empire there is no doubt, but that Alexius' investment in the First Crusade, which shattered the Seljuk power in Asia Minor and restored these regions to Byzantine rule, was an immensely profitable one is equally indubitable.

We know that the Franks appeared to the Greeks as a turbulent, fickle, and loquacious army of barbarians, possessed of an avarice would lead any one of them to sell his own wife and children, if there was anything valuable to be gained by it. One must admit that the Crusaders gave some cause for this belief. [137] It is equally true that the Franks in their passage through the Byzantine Empire were guilty of looting and of worse forms of violence, although Bohemond, for one, attempted to reduce such disorders to a minimum. It would not be difficult, however, to find in modern history examples of the mistreatment of a not unfriendly civilian population by infinitely better disciplined troops, and one may be permitted to believe that Byzantine troops campaigning, say, against the Saracens of Sicily would have distinguished themselves by very little more restraint in their treatment of the native Latin population. It must not be forgotten also that if the Greeks did not trust the Franks, the Franks were equally suspicious of the Greeks. For centuries the West had believed that the Greeks were cowardly, effeminate, and devious and treacherous in their dealings, [138] and it cannot be denied that their share in the First Crusade was by no means a glorious one.

Chalandon is entirely mistaken in his attempt to show that the Crusaders were the mercenaries of Alexius. They were, as we have seen, his vassals, and the agreement which existed between them, if not a *foedus aequum*, at least placed obligations on both parties to it. The grants to the leaders and the bestowal of alms upon the poor folk of the army must not be looked upon as payment for services to be

---

136. *Ibid.*, p. 214.

137. Anna, 2, pp. 273-276.

138. Even William of Tyre, who spent the greater part of his life in the Orient, was unable to understand the deviousness of the Greeks. "... *tandem post innumeras dilationes, et verborum aenigmata, qualiter Graeci, quaelibet cavillantes, perplexis ambagibus respondere solent, pro votis impetrant.*" WT, p. 587.

rendered, but rather as gifts made by the *basileus* in order to keep the Crusaders well-disposed toward him. If Alexius furnished markets, it must be recognized that the Crusaders paid for their own food, and did not receive it gratis from the *basileus*.

Let us now consider the most important question of all. Did Alexius and the Greeks fulfil all of their engagements towards the Crusaders and was it the latter who were responsible for the first breach in the agreement?

I have already shown that neither Bohemond nor any of the other Franks was responsible for the flight of Taticius, and that his defection was caused undoubtedly by his own cowardice.[139] The past relations of the Franks and the Greeks and the situation of the Crusaders in February, 1098, must be borne in mind in order to realize the probable effect of Taticius' desertion upon the attitude of the Crusaders toward the Greeks. Alexius had not seen fit to accompany the Franks on their dangerous march across Asia Minor. The restoration of Greek power in Asia Minor, in the words of Chalandon, "was the most immediate end which political wisdom recommended to the *basileus*,"[140] and he remained behind to garner the fruits of conquest which the victories of the Franks, won with so much peril and hardship, had dropped into his lap.

There is something not very glorious about the spectacle, and although Chalandon exclaims at Gibbon's comparison of Alexius to the bird which follows the lion to feed upon the remains of his kill,[141] one is forced to admit that the comparison is not an inapt one. The Greek authorities had supplied the Crusaders before Antioch with food, but only in miserable doles, and in February, 1098, the Franks were on starvation rations. Given this state of affairs, one can well imagine that the numbers of the anti-Greek faction, which already existed in the crusading army, were increased by the desertion of Taticius.

In spite of their disappointed hopes of Greek military aid, the crusading chiefs remained admirably loyal to their oath to Alexius, and with disaster staring them in the face, they were willing to promise Antioch to Bohemond, only on the condition that the *basileus* did not carry out his agreement. We know how Alexius fulfilled his promise by turning back from Philomelium when he learned of the dangers which menaced the Crusaders at Antioch. On exactly the occasion

---

139. See *supra.*, this chapter.
140. Chalandon, Alexis, p. 195.
141. *Ibid.*, p. 155, n. 1.

when his aid is most needed, he fails the Crusaders, because there is an element of danger involved in the expedition. It is quite true that he was forced to act upon the inaccurate information brought to him by Stephen of Blois, information which exaggerated the desperate straits of the Crusaders, but Guy and the other Latins were willing to advance to Antioch in spite of Stephen's rumours of disaster. Only the Greeks hung back. It must be borne in mind that Alexius must have known at the time that the loss of Antioch to the Greeks was likely to be the result of his defection, for Stephen and the other fugitives from Antioch undoubtedly informed him that the Crusaders had promised the city to Bohemond on condition that Alexius did not fulfil his obligations toward them. Realizing this, the *basileus* still refused to take the road to Antioch.

After the capture of Antioch and the defeat of Kerboga, the Crusaders still respected their oaths to Alexius although they had waited for his aid in vain and probably knew of his retreat from Philomelium. In spite of their promise to Bohemond, they sent Hugh of Vermandois to Constantinople, asking the *basileus* to come to receive Antioch and fulfil the rest of his obligations. Throughout the summer and the autumn the Crusaders waited without result for some word from Alexius, but in the November negotiations over the disposition of the city, the majority of the leaders, anxious to observe their obligations to the *basileus*, were still unwilling officially to hand over the city to Bohemond.

No word seems to have been received from Constantinople until the appearance of the Byzantine legates at Arka. Chalandon curiously regards the refusal of the Crusaders to wait two months longer for the arrival of Alexius as a breach of their agreement. [142] The best answer to the argument is to be found in the words of the Crusaders themselves who pointed out that the *basileus* had failed them time and time again, and now that the greatest danger was past and Jerusalem would soon be taken, Alexius was willing to put in an appearance. Why should they trust his word again?

Chalandon would have it that the political struggle of Bohemond with Alexius was the real cause of Alexius' bad reputation among the Westerners. [143] I believe that he is mistaken. All of the original historians of the First Crusade are strongly anti-Greek in their tendency, Raymond of Agiles, the chaplain of Raymond of Toulouse, and no

---

142. Chalandon, *Alexis*, p. 214.
143. *Ibid.*, p. 116.

lover of Bohemond, being especially violent in his animus against Alexius.

The anti-Greek feeling in the crusading army is distinctly percep- tible in the letter which the leaders addressed to the pope on Septem- ber 11, 1098. "We have defeated the Turks and pagans," says the letter, "but we have not been able to defeat the heretics, the Greeks and Ar- menians, Syrians and Jacobites." A postscript to the letter, which is not found in all of the manuscripts, but which Hagenmeyer, the latest edi- tor of the letter, regards as genuine, reveals an even stronger animosity against the Greeks. The pope ought to come to release the Crusaders from their oath to the *basileus*, who has promised much but in no wise fulfilled his promises, for he has done all that he could to injure and impede them. [144] The postscript, which may not have been endorsed by all of the leaders, is probably the work of Bohemond and of the faction, composed of a majority of the chiefs, which later rejected the requests of the Byzantine legates at Arka.

To sum up the argument: not Bohemond nor any other of the Crusaders but Alexius himself is responsible for the breach between the Greeks and the Franks. He was amply repaid for whatever aid he gave the Westerners by the recovery of Asia Minor. In carrying out his share of the bargain, he followed a selfish and inglorious policy, which had for its end the recovery of a maximum of territory at a minimum expenditure of aid to the Crusaders.

We need be under no illusions as to the scruples of Bohemond. The self-seeking Norman would undoubtedly have kept Antioch, if he could, promise or no promise, but it was only Alexius' policy with its repeated sins of omission that led the crusading chiefs to regard their obligations as at an end and caused them to leave the city in the hands of their resourceful comrade.

---

144. HEp, pp. 164–165.

CHAPTER 6

Bohemond, Prince of Antioch,
1099–1104

After the expulsion of the *Provençal* troops from Antioch, Bohemond remained as sole master of the city, and took the title of prince of Antioch. [1] Although the boundaries of the principality were not yet clearly defined, it is possible to indicate here in general fashion the extent of the new Norman dominions. As viewed in the large, they consisted of two parts, Cilicia and northern Syria, almost at right angles to each other, and including in the angle formed by their shores the north-eastern corner of the Mediterranean. The possession of Cilicia with its friendly Armenian population was of vital importance to the new Latin state, for the control of its passes prevented the Greeks from pouring down their troops into the indefensible plains of northern Syria, [2] while Tarsus, Mamistra, Adana, and Ainzarba were all cities of first or second-rate importance.

The county of Edessa under the lordship of Baldwin, the brother of Godfrey, protected a large part of the Antiochian front to the northeast, but to the east, nothing but the fertile and populous Syrian plain was interposed between Antioch and the emirate of Aleppo, [3] which, under a ruler of mediocre ability, was fortunately too weak to attack successfully the newly-founded Norman principality. To the south lay the fortresses of the Assassins, [4] that strange and terrible Mohammedan sect, and the Greek ports of Laodicea, Valania, and Maraclea, which,

---

1. William of Tyre is, of course, incorrect in his statement that Bohemond took the title of prince because he had used it in his own country. WT, p. 275.
2. Schlumberger, *Nicéphore Phocas*, pp. 160-161.
3. Ibn Butlân, in Le Strange, p. 370.
4. Ibn Jubair, in Le Strange, p. 78.

conquered by the Crusaders, had been handed over, as we have seen, by Raymond of Toulouse to the Greeks.

We know very little, next to nothing, about the internal conditions of the principality. It would be interesting to ascertain what arrangements were made by Bohemond with the masters of the fortresses which had been captured and manned by the Lotharingians and Provençals, but the sources give us but slight help. In all probability, these lords remained in northern Syria and continued to hold their possessions. [5] The principality was thus from the very beginning by no means an entirely Norman state. It is fruitless to attempt to estimate the number of Crusaders who remained at Antioch. Many members of Bohemond's expedition, including Tancred and the author of the *Gesta Francorum*, went on to Jerusalem under other leaders. A considerable number, however, must have remained in Syria to have enabled Bohemond to hold the country against the attacks of Greek and Turk, and this army was temporarily augmented by the yearly pilgrimages from the West and by troops from Bohemond's Italian possessions. [6]

The majority of the population of the principality was probably Christian,—Greek, Armenian, and Syrian. While Antioch itself did not suffer such a massacre as Jerusalem experienced when it was captured, a great number of its Mohammedan inhabitants were either killed or driven from the city. The plague in the summer of 1098 also carried off many more Antiochians, both Christian and Mohammedan. The villages and rural districts to the east along the shifting Aleppan boundary were undoubtedly largely Mohammedan.

It is a fair land, this country about Antioch, as the Arab travellers and geographers of the Middle Ages picture it for us, a land of marvellous fertility and prosperity, its fields yellow with the ripening wheat and barley, [7] its orchards black with olive, fig and pistachio trees [8] or colourful with the orange and citron. [9] "The villages [between Aleppo and Antioch] ran continuous," writes Ibn Butlân, "their gardens full of flowers, and the waters flowing on every hand, so that the traveller makes his journey here in contentment of mind, and peace and

---

5. Raim., p. 267.
6. Anna, 2, p. 121; Galterius Cancellarius, *Bella Antiochena*, edited by Heinrich Hagenmeyer (Innsbruck, 1896), p. 63.
7. Ibn Butlân, in Le Strange, p. 370. At the end of the eleventh century, the yield from the grain lands around Antioch alone was valued at fifteen thousand gold pieces. Behâ ed-Dîn, *The Life of Saladin* (London, 1897).
8. Ibn Jubair, in Le Strange, p. 495.
9. Mas'üdi, *ibid.*, p. 17.

quietness." [10] The air was filled with the clack of the wheels along the Orontes raising the river-water into the gardens and orchards, [11] and redolent with the fragrance of the Aleppan pine on the hillsides. [12]

The campaigns about Antioch may have shattered, at least temporarily, this picture of perfect peace and prosperity, but the country was still eminently desirable, and one can understand the anxiety of Alexius to recover it.

Having failed to obtain Antioch through diplomatic negotiations, the *basileus* now resorted to open war, and sent an army under Butumites and Monastras into Cilicia. The Armenians of the province, however, remained loyal to the Normans, and the expedition accomplished little save the occupation of Marash and the surrounding region in the mountains of Armenia. [13]

Bohemond in the meanwhile had laid siege to Laodicea, the most important sea-port in northern Syria, and so located that as long as it remained in Greek hands it would be a continual menace to the safety and integrity of the Latin principality. A Pisan fleet of one hundred twenty vessels bearing Daimbert, the new papal legate, arrived most opportunely at Laodicea in the late summer, and having already attacked the islands off the western coast of Greece and fought an indecisive battle with a Greek fleet between Rhodes and Patras, was not averse to aiding Bohemond in his siege of Laodicea. [14]

The commanders of the Greek fleet, after holding a conference at Cyprus, sent Butumites to Laodicea in an attempt to negotiate a peace with Bohemond. Butumites remained at Laodicea for two weeks but failed to come to terms with the prince of Antioch, who finally dismissed him, after charging him with having come not to make peace but to spy on the Normans and to burn their ships. The Greek fleet then returned to Constantinople.

The Greek campaigns against Antioch had been a failure, and the only accomplishment of the year, in addition to the capture of Marash, was the

---

10. Ibn Butlân, *ibid.*, p. 370.

11. Ibn Butlân, *ibid.*, p. 375.

12. Harry C. Lukach (Luke) *The Fringe of the East* (London, 1913). For other modern descriptions of the same region, see Karl Baedeker, *Palestine and Syria* (Leipzig, 1912); Vital Cuinet, *La Turquie d'Asie* (Paris, 1892), 2, pp. 134-142; William H. Hall, *Antioch the Glorious, in the National Geographic Magazine*, 38, pp. 81-103.

13. Anna, 2, pp. 113-1 15. In spite of Anna's reference to Tancred's presence at Antioch, I agree with Kugler in placing these events in 1099 and not in 1103.

14. *Gesta triumphalia Pisanorum in captione Hierosolymae*, in *Rec. Hist, occ.*, 5, p. 368; Anna 2, pp. 115-119; Alb., p. 511.

fortification of Seleucia and Curicius on the south-eastern coast of Isauria almost due west of the Port of St. Simeon. Greek men-of-war were stationed at Curicius as a menace to Syrian-bound fleets from the West. [15]

Meanwhile, Bohemond's siege of Laodicea was progressing satisfactorily. A number of towers were captured by the land forces, while the Pisan fleet performed invaluable service in investing and bombarding the city from the harbour. An unexpected check, however, appeared in September in the shape of Raymond of Toulouse, who in the company of Robert of Normandy and Robert of Flanders and a host of returning Crusaders had marched north after the capture of Jerusalem and the defeat of the Egyptians at Ascalon. We can only conjecture what motives brought back to northern Syria the fierce old *Provençal* count, who had sworn never to return to the West. Perhaps it was the desire to undertake fresh conquests south of Antioch or to commune with the imperial representatives in the region.

The returning Crusaders learned of the siege of Laodicea at Jabala, possibly from Greek legates sent by the Laodiceans, [16] and meeting Daimbert between Jabala and Laodicea, they, or at least Raymond, the friend of Alexius, reproached him for having aided Bohemond in an attack upon a Christian city. The papal legate excused himself by explaining that Bohemond had led him to believe that the Laodiceans were enemies of the Crusaders and that it was under this misapprehension that the Pisans had cooperated in the attack upon the city. He then returned to Laodicea, accompanied by representatives of the crusading leaders, and attempted to induce Bohemond to give up his designs upon the city. His efforts were fruitless, and it was only after Daimbert had withdrawn the support of the Pisan fleet that Bohemond gave up the siege and moved his camp a half-mile from the city.

On arriving at Laodicea the next day, Raymond was admitted to the city and raised his banner on the highest tower. Some days later, Bohemond and Raymond were reconciled by Daimbert and adjusted their differences. The two Roberts then took ship for Constantinople, while Raymond remained at Laodicea and Bohemond, according to Albert of Aachen, returned to Antioch three days after he had made peace with Raymond. [17] We cannot be entirely sure of his movements,

---

15. Anna, 2, pp. 119–121.

16. Ord., 4, pp. 71–72.

17. Alb., pp. 500–504; *Epistula (Dagoberti) Pisani archiepiscopi et Godefridi ducis et Raimundi de S. Aegidii et universi exercitus in terra Israel ad papam et omnes Christi fideles,* in HEp, p. 173; HE, pp. 183–186; Ord 4, pp. 71–75.

however, for he seems to have joined Raymond and the Pisans in an attack upon Jabala. [18] Neither Bohemond and his followers nor Baldwin and his contingent at Edessa had as yet fulfilled their crusading vows. Anxious to visit Jerusalem, therefore, and absolve his vows, Bohemond wrote to Baldwin in the autumn, proposing a joint expedition to the Holy City. [19] Baldwin acquiesced, and in November joined Bohemond, whom he found lying before Valania. Although the sources are silent on this question, we may conjecture that Bohemond had attempted to capture this Greek seaport on his way south. The expedition, according to Fulk, was a large one, and included five bishops in addition to Daimbert—an Apulian bishop who cannot be identified, Roger of Tarsus, Bartholomew of Mamistra, Bernard of Artah, and Benedict of Edessa. [20]

The pilgrims, after suffering terribly from hunger and cold on the journey, arrived in Jerusalem on December 21. They made the usual round of the holy places, visiting the Sepulchre and the Temple and going to Bethlehem where they spent Christmas Eve. They returned to Jerusalem on Christmas Day. [21] Probably on the same day Daimbert was elected patriarch of Jerusalem with the assistance of Bohemond, [22] the four bishops from Antioch and Edessa were consecrated, [23] and Bohemond and Godfrey, the latter now Baron and Defender of the Holy Sepulchre, received their possessions as fiefs from Daimbert. [24]

What motives led the prince of Antioch to support Daimbert for election to the patriarchate and to become his vassal? Kugler and Kühne have seen in Bohemond's actions an evidence of his far-reaching designs upon Jerusalem and Palestine. Tancred, according to Kugler, accompanied the expedition to Jerusalem chiefly as Bohemond's agent, in an effort to gain a foot-hold for Norman power in the south, and Bohemond raised up Daimbert to the patriarchate in order to prevent the growth of a strong Lotharingian monarchy in Palestine, since the Pisan was a man of strong hierarchical views. [25]

---

18. *Gesta triumphalia Pisanorum*, p. 369.

19. HF, p. 325.

20. *Ibid.*, pp. 325-328; Rad., p. 704.

21. HF, pp. 328-332.

22. *Ibid.*, p. 333; Alb., p. 512; Rad., p. 704; Bartolf., p. 519.

23. Rad., p. 704.

24. HF, pp. 741-742. See WT, pp. 387; 405-406.

25. Kugler, *Boemund und Tankred*, pp. n, 14-15, 62-63; Ernst Kühne, *Zur Geschichte des Fürstentums Antiochia, I, Unter normannischer Herrschaft* (1098-1130), *Programm* (Berlin, 1897), pp. 7-8.

The hypothesis is an ingenious one and yet slight evidence can be found for it in the sources. One is led to wonder why Bohemond should have concerned himself with Jerusalem and Palestine when he had not yet made full use of his opportunities in the fertile and populous Syria. The population of Jerusalem had been depleted by the terrible massacre which accompanied its capture, while Palestine itself was less productive and much less securely held at this date than the principality of Antioch. Even the greedy and ambitious Raymond of Toulouse had refused the office of Baron and Defender of the Holy Sepulchre. [26]

As for Tancred's part in the conquest of Palestine, there is no evidence to support Kugler's statement that he was acting chiefly in the interests of Bohemond in an effort to establish a Norman *pied-à-terre* in the south. On the contrary, we know from Raymond of Agiles that Tancred received five thousand *solidi* from Raymond of Toulouse, the enemy of Bohemond, and went south in his service. [27] There is evidence enough in the sources that Tancred and his uncle were not always on the best of terms and that their ambitions not infrequently clashed. How else explain the fact that when Tancred went to Antioch in 1100 to accept the regency after his uncle's capture by the Turks, the garrison of the city denied him admittance until he had sworn to remain faithful to Bohemond? [28] And his oath notwithstanding, he concerned himself very little with his uncle's plight and seems to have done nothing to effect his release.[29] In my opinion, Tancred's participation in the campaign against Jerusalem was caused not by the desire to create a Norman sphere of influence in Palestine in Bohemond's interest, but merely by the love of adventure and the hope of conquering a portion of the land for himself. His ambitions like those of all the other leaders of the First Crusade were inspired by personal and not by national considerations.

In regard to Daimbert, if Bohemond supported his candidacy because he believed that the Pisan would prevent the growth of a strong Lotharingian state in Palestine, there is no reason for thinking that the newly-elected patriarch would not have been equally opposed to the expansion of Norman lay influence in the same region.

Bohemond's support of Daimbert and his willingness to become

26. Raim., p. 301.
27. Raim., p. 278.
28. *Hist. bel. sacr.*, p. 288.
29. See *infra*, p. 96.

the latter's vassal were caused by other considerations. What the Norman desired in 1099 was not additional territory but a good title to that which he already possessed. Alexius still laid claim to Antioch and there were undoubtedly many Latins who regarded Bohemond as a perjurer and a usurper. Bohemond had attempted to strengthen his insecure position as early as September, 1098, by begging Urban II to come and release him from his oath to the *basileus*. [30] His plea had been a vain one, and that failing, he turned to the next highest authority, the papal legate, and struck a bargain with that ambitious individual. In return for Bohemond's support of his patriarchal aspirations, Daimbert undoubtedly agreed to become the Norman's overlord. By receiving back his lands as a fief from the patriarch and papal legate, Bohemond gained what he desired a legal title to Antioch which could scarcely be challenged by any other Frank and which would receive general recognition in the Latin West.

On January 1, 1100, the army of pilgrims went to Jericho, [31] and on the fifth said farewell to Godfrey and Daimbert near the Jordan and started on their march north. [32] They passed Tiberias, Banias, Baalbek, near which they beat off a Turkish attack, and Tortosa, arriving eventually at Laodicea, where they found Raymond of Toulouse, but no food. Bohemond returned thence to Antioch, while Baldwin kept on his way to Edessa. [33]

During the next half-year, Bohemond spent his time in extending his territories to the east at the expense of the emirate of Aleppo. In May or early in June, he besieged Apamea for several days and laid waste the fields in the neighbourhood. [34] Not long afterwards, Rudwan of Aleppo marched to Atharib and set out thence to drive the Franks from Kella. The troops, however, from Jezr, Zaredna, and Sarmin, which were now in Bohemond's hands, united and inflicted a decisive defeat upon Rudwan, capturing five hundred of his troops. As a result, Kafr Haleb and Hadhir and most of the country to the west of Aleppo fell into the hands of the Franks. [35]

Bohemond now planned an attack on Aleppo itself and fitted up el–Mushrifa as a base, with the intention of living upon the surround-

30. See *supra*, chapter 5.

31. HF, p. 335.

32. Alb., p. 512.

33. HF, pp. 335–343; Rad., p. 704.

34. Ibn el–Athîr, p. 204.

35. Kamal-ad-Din, p. 588; Sibt ibn el-Jeuzi, *Mirât ez Zèmân*, in *Rec., Hist, or.*, 3, p.522.

ing country. [36] According to the Arab historians, he was still near Aleppo when messengers arrived from Gabriel, the governor of Malatia, an Armenian city far to the north. Gabriel begged for aid against Kumushtakin ibn Danishmend, *emir* of Sirvas, who was besieging Malatia. [37] According to Matthew of Edessa, Bohemond was besieging Marash when he received the plea for aid. [38] At all events he set out for the besieged city with a relief expedition insufficient in size. [39] Advancing incautiously on Malatia, the Franks fell into an ambush which had been prepared for them by Kumushtakin, and were put to flight almost without a struggle. Bohemond and his cousin, Richard of the Principate, less fortunate than their companions, were taken captive by the Turks.

While Kumushtakin continued his siege of Malatia, Bohemond found an opportunity to communicate with Baldwin of Edessa, and sent him a lock of his hair, a not unusual symbol of distress during the Middle Ages. [40] Hastily collecting an army of Edessans and enlisting the aid of the survivors of the Turkish ambush, who had probably made their way into the county of Edessa, Baldwin marched on Malatia, but learning of his approach, Kumushtakin raised the siege and fled north with his captives, pursued by Baldwin for three days. Unable to overtake the enemy, the Franks returned sadly home, while Kumushtakin conducted his prisoners to Nixandria (ancient Neocaesarea, modern Niksar), far in the north of Asia Minor, where he threw them into chains. The Turks were overjoyed at the capture of the great prince of Antioch, "for," says Matthew of Edessa, "the infidels regarded Bohemond as the real sovereign of the Franks, and his name made all Khorasan tremble." [41] The capture took place probably in the month of July or early in August, 1100. [42]

In the meanwhile, the new Latin state in Palestine had been torn by a great internal struggle, a struggle which would surely have involved the prince of Antioch had he not been captured by the Turks. Our sources for these events are unsatisfactory for we have only Albert and William of Tyre.

---

36. Kamal-ad-Din, p. 589.
37. *Ibid.*: Sibt ibn el-Jeuzi, p. 522.
38. Matthieu d'Edesse, pp. 50-51.
39. HF, pp. 344-345.
40. HF, pp. 347-348 and p. 348, n. 15.
41. Matthieu d'Edesse, p. 52.
42. HF, pp. 343-349; Matthieu d'Edesse, pp. 50-52; Alb., pp. 524-525; Ord., 4, p. 140; Kamal-ad-Din, p. 589; Ibn el-Athîr, p. 203; Sibt ibn el-Jeuzi, p. 522.

According to Albert's account, at Godfrey's death on July 18, 1100, Daimbert and Tancred conspired to prevent Baldwin of Edessa, designated by his brother, Godfrey, as his successor, from obtaining the state of Jerusalem, and ignorant of Bohemond's capture, sent Morellus, the patriarch's secretary, to him with a letter, asking him to kill Baldwin on the latter's way to Jerusalem and to come himself to be recognized as ruler of the state. The message never reached Antioch, for Morellus fell into the hands of the *Provençal* garrison of Laodicea,[43] and the letter came eventually into the hands of Baldwin.[44]

William of Tyre, who used Albert as a source, but who seems to have also had other sources of information on this point, tells a somewhat similar but less-detailed story, and adds a document which purports to be the original text of Daimbert's letter to Bohemond. The patriarch begins by acknowledging the aid he received from Bohemond in his election to the patriarchate, then enumerates the grants which Godfrey had made to him before his death, and recounts how the Lotharingians have invaded his rights by occupying the Tower of David and sending to Edessa for Baldwin; he reminds Bohemond of his promise of aid and of his obligations to St. Peter, and begs the prince of Antioch to help him now, as his father, Guiscard, once helped Gregory VII. Let him write to Baldwin and exhort him not to go to Jerusalem; if this does not suffice, let him use other means, force, if necessary, to check the Lotharingian.[45]

Is the letter genuine or not? Scores of pages have been written on the subject,[46] but it is obvious from a study of the question that it cannot be settled conclusively, from lack of both the necessary internal and external evidence. Even if it could be proved that the letter is a forgery or one of William's elucubrations, the question as to whether Daimbert ever begged aid of Bohemond against Baldwin would still be undecided.

William's version differs from Albert's in one important respect. Daimbert's letter, as the archbishop gives it, conveys no invitation to Bohemond to come to Jerusalem to be made ruler of Palestine. I do not doubt from the evidence of Albert and the partly independent

43. Albert says that Morellus was captured by Raymond, which is impossible for the count had left Laodicea for Constantinople about the middle of May. HChr, no. 460.
44. Alb., pp. 524, 538-539.
45. WT, pp. 404-406.
46. For the literature on Daimbert's letter, see Reinhold Röhricht, *Geschichte des Königreichs Jerusalem*. (Innsbruck, 1898), p. 7, n. 1.

William that Daimbert sought to enlist the aid of Bohemond against the Lotharingians, but I much prefer the account of William to that of Albert. Why should Daimbert offer to make Bohemond king of Jerusalem or even baron and defender of the Holy Sepulchre? Daimbert wanted not merely to change the ruling dynasty of Jerusalem, but to convert the country into a church-state with himself as ruler. The permanent presence in Palestine of the ambitious Bohemond would have proved every whit as embarrassing to Daimbert's plans as that of Baldwin. We may be sure then that when the patriarch called upon Bohemond for aid he did so not by holding out to Bohemond the hope of becoming lay ruler of Palestine, but under the terms of the oath of vassalage which Bohemond had taken to him.

But let us return to a consideration of Antioch. Fortunately for that state, Raymond of Toulouse was no longer at Laodicea when Bohemond was captured, for he had left for Constantinople in May. [47] Realizing their weakness without a leader, the people of Antioch sent legates to Tancred, asking him to come and act as regent during his uncle's captivity. If we are to believe Albert of Aachen, the regency had already been offered to and refused by Baldwin of Edessa, while he was sojourning at Antioch on his way to Jerusalem. [48] Tancred's acceptance of the regency must then have occurred subsequent to Baldwin's refusal, and this is confirmed by the statement of *Historia belli sacri* that Tancred turned aside on his way to Antioch to avoid meeting his old rival, Baldwin. [49]

Tancred seems to have accepted the regency and gone north promptly, but on arriving at Antioch, he found himself denied admittance to the city, until he swore to remain faithful to Bohemond. [50] He was duly invested with the regency, Maurice, the new papal legate, and the other leading men from the Genoese fleet which had put into Laodicea for the winter, assisting at the ceremony. [51] After his investiture, Tancred returned to Palestine to look after his possessions there. In March, 1101, messengers from Antioch arrived in the kingdom, begging him not to absent himself any longer. Handing over his fiefs to Baldwin, now ruler of Jerusalem, on the condition that they should be restored to him if he returned within a year and three months,

47 See *supra*, p. 93.
48. Alb., p. 537.
49. *Hist. bel. sacr.*, p. 228; Alb., p. 532.
50. *Hist . bel. sacr.*, p. 228.
51. Cafarus, *Annales Ianuenses*, MGSS, 18, p. 11.

Tancred departed for Antioch. [52]

The people of Antioch were singularly fortunate in their choice of a regent as subsequent events were to show, for Tancred, during his uncle's captivity, not only kept the principality intact, but recovered lost territory and conquered new. Soon after his arrival, he reconquered Tarsus, Adana, and Mamistra which had been occupied by the Greeks some time before. [53] After capturing Apamea, he laid siege to Laodicea, probably in 1102, and after a year and a half received its surrender. [54]

In 1102, the survivors of the luckless Crusade of 1101 reached Antioch where they were entertained, and Tancred captured and imprisoned Raymond of Toulouse, ostensibly on the grounds that, acting as the tool of Alexius, he had betrayed the crusading armies in Asia Minor, [55] but really because Tancred knew that the count, in accordance with his agreement with the *basileus*, was on his way to begin a series of conquests to the south of Antioch. Forced to release him at last at the solicitation of Bernard, the Latin patriarch, the clergy, and the crusading leaders, he first exacted from him the oath that he would attempt no conquests between Antioch and Acre. [56] Suffice it to say that Raymond did not keep his oath.

We know practically nothing of Tancred's campaigns against the Turks during Bohemond's captivity. They were probably of small proportions, for Antioch now lacked the cooperation of Edessa, due to the unfriendliness existing between Tancred and Baldwin of Bourg, who had succeeded Baldwin of Lorraine as count of Edessa in 1100.[57]

With all of his activity, Tancred seems to have done nothing to bring about his uncle's release from captivity. Kumushtakin must have allowed Bohemond to remain in communication with the Franks, for, according to Ralph of Caen and Ordericus Vitalis, Bernard was appointed patriarch of Antioch by Bohemond from his prison in Asia Minor, [58] and if we are to believe Albert, the illustrious captive was permitted to send to Antioch and Edessa and even to Sicily in his at-

---

52. Alb., p. 538; HF, pp. 390-393.
53. Rad., p. 706.
54. *Ibid.*, pp. 706-709 ; WT, p. 435; Anna, 2, p. 107.
55. Alb., p. 582. According to Albert, p. 563, the Crusaders in the expedition of 1101 had planned to rescue Bohemond.
56. Alb., pp. 582-583; Rad., pp. 707-708; Matthieu d'Edesse, pp. 57-58.
57. WT, pp. 435-436; Rad., pp. 706, 709.
58. Rad., p. 709; Ord., 4, p. 142.

tempts to raise his ransom.[59]

Due to the generosity of the patriarch, Bernard, Baldwin of Bourg,[60] and Kogh Vasil, the Armenian lord of Kasun, who advanced ten thousand gold pieces and conducted the negotiations with Kumushtakin,[61] the ransom of one hundred thousand gold pieces[62] was at length collected and paid in 1103. Tancred contributed not a penny.[63] After he had promised to release the daughter of Yagi Siyan, who was still a prisoner among the Franks,[64] and had probably made some sort of treaty with Kumushtakin,[65] Bohemond was at length released. He was entertained for several days by Kogh Vasil and adopted as his son,[66] and then returned in the summer of 1103 to Antioch,[67] where, after his three years of captivity, he was received with great joy. With him returned Richard of the Principate.[68]

A number of legends dealing with the subject of Bohemond's captivity and release, and partially founded on fact, sprang up within a very short time.

According to Albert of Aachen, Alexius, anxious to get possession of Bohemond, offered Kumushtakin 260,000 gold Michaels for him; on Kumushtakin's refusal to promise part of the ransom to Kilij Arslan, the latter attacked and defeated him. Bohemond then advised his captor to reject Alexius' offer and to release him on the payment of one hundred thousand gold pieces and the promise of his friendship; Kumushtakin acquiesced, set the Norman free, and afterwards rejected Kilij Arslan's proposal to recapture Bohemond by means of a treacherous ruse.[69]

There may be some truth in Albert's story, for Ordericus Vitalis also mentions that the *basileus* offered a hundred thousand gold pieces for Bohemond and that the *emir* refused to surrender the "Little God

---

59. Alb., p. 613.

60. Rad., p. 709. Ralph implies that Baldwin's zeal in Bohemond's behalf was caused by his hatred of Tancred.

61. Matthieu d'Edesse, pp. 69-70.

62. *Ibid.*; Alb., p. 612; Ibn el-Athîr, p. 212.

63. Matthieu d'Edesse, p. 69.

64. Ibn el-Athîr, p. 212; Ord., 4, p. 153.

65. Alb., pp. 611-612; Guib., p. 254.

66. Matthieu d'Edesse, p. 70.

67. Albert, p. 614, indicates May as the date of Bohemond's release, but places it incorrectly in 1104.

68. Matthieu d'Edesse, p. 70.

69. Alb., pp. 610-614.

of the Christians." [70] Orderic then follows this account with a very fanciful story of Bohemond's captivity. Melaz, Kumushtakin's beautiful daughter, visits the prisoners frequently and hearing them speak of their religion decides to espouse Christianity herself. While her father is absent on a campaign against Kilij Arslan, Melaz releases Bohemond and his companions, who follow Kumushtakin, or Dolimannus, as he is called in the story, aid him in defeating Kilij Arslan, and then return, lock up the guard, and occupy their captor's citadel.

On his return, Kumushtakin, enraged at his daughter's act, threatens to kill her but is prevented by the Franks, who force him to agree to release all of his Prankish prisoners on condition that the Franks set free their Turkish prisoners. The terms are carried out, and Bohemond and his companions return with the *emir's* daughter to Antioch, where the girl is baptized. Bohemond explains that because of the arduous and dangerous existence that he leads and the necessity of returning to the West to fulfil a vow, it would be inadvisable for him to marry her. He, therefore, betroths her to Roger, the son of Richard of the Principate, and acts himself as master of the ceremonies at the wedding which takes place amid the rejoicing of all Antioch.[71]

Still another story of Bohemond's captivity is to be found in the collection of the miracles of St. Leonard of Noblac, the authorship of which is probably incorrectly assigned to Waleran, bishop of Nürnberg. [72] Poncelet, in a study of the question, has established a probability that the story is based on his own account of his adventures which Bohemond gave during his sojourn in France in 1106. [73]

According to the legend, the prisoners are befriended by Kumushtakin's wife, who is secretly a Christian, and are furnished by her with food and clothing. Richard is at length released through the intercession of St. Leonard, while the same saint informs Bohemond in a dream of his approaching release. Kumushtakin, defeated by Kilij Arslan, is advised by his wife, to whom St. Leonard has appeared, to release his captive; he at first rejects her advice, but thinks better of it, and agrees to set Bohemond free on condition of the payment of a small ransom and the promise of an alliance with him. The Turks

70. Ord., 4, pp. 140-141. Cf. Matthieu d'Edesse, p. 70, who mentions negotiations of Alexius with Kumushtakin for the person of Richard of the Principate.

71. Ord., 4, pp. 144-158.

72. Gaufredus Vosiensis, *Chronicon,* in Philippus Labbe, *Nova bibliotheca manuscriptorum* (Paris, 1657), 2, p. 297.

73. Albert Poncelet, *Boémond et s. Léonard, in Analecta Bollandiana,* 1912, 31, pp. 24-44.

themselves collect and pay Bohemond's ransom, and after a successful war against Kilij Arslan he returns to Antioch. [74]

It is extremely interesting to note the similarities in the three stories. The even more fanciful accounts which are to be found in later poems need not concern us here. Tancred surrendered the principality, now augmented by the capture of Laodicea, with a very bad grace. [75] His fiefs in the south had escheated to Baldwin and there was nothing left for him to do but to remain in Syria and assist his uncle in his campaigns. According to Raoul of Caen, only two small towns were left in his possession, [76] this treatment undoubtedly being the result of his failure to aid in the release of Bohemond.

Soon after his return, Bohemond, in conjunction with troops from Edessa, invaded the emirate of Aleppo, and camped at el-Muslimiya for several days, killing a number of the inhabitants and exacting tribute from the rest. A treaty was finally arranged between the Franks and Turks, under the terms of which, Rudwan agreed to pay seven thousand gold pieces and ten horses, while the Franks engaged themselves to release their Mohammedan prisoners, with the exception of the officers taken at el-Muslimiya. [77] Ibn-el Athîr also chronicles the imposition by the Franks of taxes upon the el-Awasim district and upon Kinnesrin and the surrounding country. [78] Aleppo in 1103 was plainly on the defensive.

In 1104, the Franks of northern Syria continued their operations against Aleppo. On March 29, Bohemond captured the fortress of Basarfut near Aleppo but was later repulsed before Kafr Catha. [79] Sometime later in the spring, Bohemond, at the proposal of Baldwin of Bourg, joined him in an attack on the fortress of Harran, south of Edessa. The expedition must have been an important one, for we find with it, in addition to Bohemond and Baldwin, Tancred, Joscellin of Tell-Bashir, Bernard, patriarch of Antioch, Benedict, and Daimbert, ex-patriarch of Jerusalem, who, forced to leave Jerusalem because of the hostility of King Baldwin, had come to Antioch and received the Church of St. George from Bohemond. [80]

74. *Scriptum Galeranni episcopi de miraculo Boimundi*, AASS, 6 Nov. 3, pp. 160-168.

75. Rad., p. 709; HF, pp. 459-460.

76. Rad., p. 709.

77. Kamal-ad-Din, p. 591.

78. Ibn el-Athîr, p. 212.

79. Kugler, *Boemund und Tankred*, pp. 25, 68; Röhricht, *Geschichte des Königreichs*, p. 49.

80. WT, p. 439.

The Franks, after besieging Harran for several days, learned of the approach of Sokman ibn Ortok of Maridin and Jakarmish of Mosul and marched south to meet the enemy. The armies met in May [81] on the Balikh River not far from Rakka. As Heermann has remarked, [82] it is impossible to reconstruct the course of the battle, so conflicting are the sources. His inference that the Franks were attacked while on the march seems plausible. [83] At all events, the Edessans bore the brunt of the first attack, and if Ibn el-Athîr is to be believed, they were the victims of a ruse of the Turks, who pretended to retreat and then turned upon them and crushed them, capturing Baldwin and Joscellin. [84] The army of Antioch was forced to retreat, and so closely was it pressed by the Turkish cavalry that the retreat eventually became a flight. A sally made by the garrison of Harran increased the confusion, [85] and it is probable that only a small part of the army reached Edessa with Bohemond and Tancred. Leaving Tancred as regent of Edessa in Baldwin's absence, Bohemond returned to Antioch. [86]

The failure of the Harran campaign must be ascribed to the carelessness of the Prankish leaders, and to the quarrels and divided counsels which existed among them. [87] The defeat was a heavy blow to both Antioch and Edessa; had the campaign turned out otherwise, the subsequent history of the two northern states would probably have been materially changed.

Soon after his return to Antioch, Bohemond was called to Edessa by Tancred, who was besieged by Jakarmish, but before his arrival, which was delayed by the wretched roads, Tancred had made a sally and defeated the Turks. Bohemond, meeting and attacking the retreating Mohammedans, completed the rout. [88] According to Albert, Tancred had captured a Turkish matron, whom the Turks were very anxious to recover and whom they offered to accept in exchange for Baldwin of Bourg or to ransom for fifteen thousand gold pieces. King Baldwin urged Bohemond and Tancred to effect the release of the

81. Sibt ibn el-Jeuzi, p. 527.
82. Heermann, p. 69.
83. *Ibid.*, p. 72.
84. Ibn el-Athîr, p. 221.
85. Matthieu d'Edesse, p. 73.
86. The chief sources for the campaign are the following: HF, pp. 468-477; Rad., pp. 710-712; Alb., pp. 614-616; WT, pp. 443-447; Matthieu d'Edesse, pp. 71-72; Ibn el-Athîr, pp. 221-222.
87. HF, p. 475; WT, p. 445.
88. Alb., pp. 617-619; Ibn el-Athîr, p. 223.

count of Edessa, but they replied that they were forced to prefer the ransom, since they were in great need of money with which to pay their troops, an answer, says Albert, which only served to conceal their real purpose, which was to increase their own power at the expense of Baldwin. [89]

Bohemond returned to Antioch to take up once more the work of defence against Turk and Greek. Emboldened by the success of his compatriots at Harran, Rudwan of Aleppo now undertook the reconquest of his lost territory. He summoned the inhabitants of Jezr and other towns and fortresses held by the Franks to revolt and arrest the Christians living there. As a result, Fuah. Sarmin, Maarat mesrin, and many other towns returned to Turkish power, while the Christian garrisons evacuated Latmin, Kafr tab, Marra and Barra, [90] Artah was reoccupied by the Turks, [91] and Hab remained as the only important Christian stronghold in Aleppan territory. Rudwan now felt secure enough to attack the principality of Antioch proper, and his raids were carried as far as the Iron Bridge. [92]

It was unfortunate for Bohemond that the Greeks should have chosen to attack his possessions in the same year. In the spring, probably while Bohemond was engaged in the campaign against Harran, a Greek fleet under Cantacuzenus appeared before Laodicea and occupied the harbour. On the day following Cantacuzenus began the construction of a wall to shut off the city from access to the sea, and near the wall he constructed a citadel. He also suspended a chain between two towers at the harbour entrance in order to prevent Frankish ships from entering or leaving the harbour.

During the course of the siege, the Greeks extended their operations to the south, and captured from the Turks the important ports of Argyrocastrum, Margat, and Jabala. Laodicea finally capitulated to the Greeks, although the citadel of the city with its garrison of five hundred infantry and one hundred cavalry still held out. Learning of the desperate plight of his garrison, Bohemond hastened to Laodicea with all his available forces.

After a fruitless interview with Cantacuzenus, Bohemond gave the

---

89. Alb., pp. 619-620.
90. Kamal-ad-Din, p. 592. Nothing is known of the circumstances under which Marra and Barra, which had been captured from the Turks by the Provençals, came into the hands of the Normans.
91. Rad., p. 712; Kamal-ad-Din, p. 593.
92. Kamal-ad-Din, pp. 592-593.

word for an attack upon the city which was repulsed by the Greeks. He did, however, succeed in forcing his way into the citadel which he restocked with food and garrisoned with new troops, for he had reason to suspect the loyalty of the original garrison. He then returned to Antioch.

The fortunes of Antioch became still darker when a Greek force under Monastras, which had been sent by Alexius into Cilicia to co-operate with Cantacuzenus' naval expedition, met with far-reaching successes. The Cilician cities expelled their Norman garrisons, and Monastras occupied Longinias, Tarsus, Adana, and Mamistra. [93]

Bohemond had slight resources with which to meet effectually the attack of the Turks and Greeks. With the Greeks in control of the Cilician passes and in possession of Laodicea, with Raymond of Toulouse, the ally of Alexius, daily increasing his territories to the south of the principality and the Turks pressing hard upon the eastern marches, the situation of Antioch seemed indeed a grave one. The army of Antioch had undoubtedly suffered great losses at Harran, and it was difficult to secure new troops in northern Syria. In addition, there was little money forthcoming with which to employ soldiers, and Bohemond was undoubtedly still in debt for his ransom to Kumushtakin. [94] There was nothing left for him to do but to return to the West to secure more men and money.

Summoning Tancred to Antioch and calling a council in the Church of St. Peter, Bohemond made known his decision to return to Europe, and to hand over the regency of Antioch during his absence to Tancred. To the latter's offer to go in his stead, he replied that the seriousness and importance of the mission made his own presence necessary, and he further recalled the vow which he had made during his captivity in Asia Minor to visit the tomb of St. Leonard of Limoges, the patron saint of prisoners. [95]

Leaving Tancred as ruler of Antioch and Edessa, [96] Bohemond sailed from the Port of St. Simeon (some time in the autumn of 1104),

---

93. Anna, 2, pp. 123-126; Rad., p. 712.

94. WT, p. 450; Dandulus, pp. 259-260; Suger, *Vie de Louis le Gros*, edited by Auguste Molinier (Paris, 1887), p. 135.

95. Rad., pp. 712-714; *Hist. bel. sacr.*, p. 229. According to Ordericus Vitalis, 4, p. 156, Bohemond had sent Richard of the Principate to the saint's shrine with a votive offering of silver fetters soon after his release from captivity.

96. According to Fulk of Chartres, p. 479, Bohemond exacted an oath from Tancred that he would hand back Edessa to Baldwin on the latter's release.

with a fleet of thirteen ships, [97] and in company with Daimbert and Frederick of Zimmern. [98] Evading the Greek fleet, he landed safely at Bari in January, 1105.[99]

Little is known of the institutions or internal conditions of the principality of Antioch under Bohemond.

The first Latin prince of Antioch seems to have lived on friendly terms with the Church. According to Ordericus Vitalis, both he and Tancred respected and confirmed the possessions of the Greek, Armenian, and Syrian monastic orders. [100] John IV, the Greek patriarch of Antioch, [101] whom the Crusaders found in it when they captured it in 1098, remained at Antioch until 1100, and the Franks, considering that it was uncanonical that there should be two patriarchs for one chair, refrained from electing a Latin patriarch. [102] About the time of Bohemond's capture, John, seeing little profit in being Greek patriarch of a Latin state, returned to Constantinople, and Bernard, bishop of Artah, was elected Latin patriarch of Antioch through the favour of Bohemond. [103] The quarrels between Church and State which were so common in the kingdom of Jerusalem were almost unknown in Antioch, and Bernard seems to have cooperated loyally with Bohemond and his successors.

Antioch, like the other Latin states in the East, had no fleet worth mentioning, and like the kingdom and Tripoli, was dependent upon the Italian maritime cities for assistance at sea. A Genoese fleet rendered valuable aid to the Crusaders during the siege of Antioch, [104] and again in 1100-1101, the Genoese fleet which wintered at Laodicea reconquered from the Turks many of the fortresses in the vicinity.[105]

---

97. *Hist. bel. sacr.*, p. 228. These were probably Genoese ships.

98 .Heinrich Hagenmeyer, *Etude sur la chronique de Zimmern*, in *Archives de l'Orient latin*, 1884, 2, pp. 29-30; HF, pp. 465-467. 99. *An. Bar. Chron.*, p. 155; *Hist. bel. sacr.*, p. 228. Romuald of Salerno, p. 413, places the return in December, 1104. Anna's account of Bohemond's return is undoubtedly fiction. Anna, 2, pp. 126-130; Chalandon, *Alexis*, p. 236, n. 6.

100. Ord., 4, p. 77.

101. For John IV, see Michel le Quien, *Oriens Christianus in IV patriarchatus digestus* (Paris, 1740), 2, cols. 756-757.

102. WT, p. 274.

103. Rad., p. 709; Ord. IV, pp. 141-142; WT, p. 274. William, who is dating the event from the capture of Antioch, says John left Antioch "*vix evoluto biennio*," which would place his departure in 1100. Mas Latrie errs in placing Bernard's election in 1100. L. de Mas Latrie, *Les patriarches latins d'Antioche*, in ROL, 1894, 2, p. 193.

104. Cafarus, *De liberatione*, p. 50.

105. Cafarus, *Annales Ianuenses*, p. 12.

The Pisans were of assistance to Bohemond in the siege of Laodicea in 1099, [106] while the Venetian fleet touched at one of the Antiochian ports in 1100. [107]

The aid of these fleets was purchased, of course, with valuable commercial and territorial concessions. We have already noted the grant of Bohemond to the Genoese of July 14, 1098.[108] A grant by Tancred to the Genoese, dated 1101, confirmed the grant of Bohemond of 1098, and added a third of the returns of the Port of St. Simeon, and the promise of half of the returns of Laodicea and a quarter in that city and in all the other cities taken with the assistance of the Genoese. Tancred promised, in addition, to the Church of St. Lawrence in Genoa a warehouse in Jabala and a *vill* outside the city, and pledged himself to see that justice was done promptly to all Genoese in his territories. [109]

A grant of Reginald of Antioch, dated May, 1153, confirms the privileges granted to the Venetians by Bohemond I and his successors.[110]

A document of Roger of Antioch confirms the grant of three *casalia* in the mountains of Antioch made by Bohemond to the Hospital at Jerusalem. [111]

There are two coins in existence, the first of which is almost certainly, and the second very probably to be ascribed to Bohemond. The first is a copper coin of Byzantine type, bearing on the obverse the bust of St. Peter, with his right hand raised in benediction, and holding a cross in his left; the coin bears the words ὁ πέτρος ; the reverse has a cross and the letters B-M-H-T, undoubtedly the abbreviation for some Greek form of the name, Bohemond. The coin, according

106. See *supra*, this chapter.

107. Adolf Schaube, *Handelsgeschichte der romanischen Völker des Mittelmeergebiets bis zum Ende der Kreuzzüge* (Munich and Berlin, 1906) p.126.

108. See *supra*, chapter 5.

109. Ughelli, 4, cols. 847-848. This grant exists only in a mutilated form. In the sentence beginning "*Et secunda pars portus Laodiciae maris, et terrae,*" I have interjected the word, "*redituum,*" between "*pars*" and "*portus.*" A comparison of the document with the confirmations of 1127 and 1169 will justify my emendation. *Liber iurium reipublicae Genuensis,* in *Historiae patriae monumenta* (Turin, 1854), 1, cols. 30-31; Ughelli, 4, cols. 871-872.

110. G. L. F. Tafel and G. M. Thomas, *Urkunden zur älteren Handels und Staatsgeschichte der Republik Venedig mit besonderer Beziehung auf Byzanz und die Levante,* in *Fontes rerum Austriacarum, zweite Abtheilung,* 1, p. 133.

111. Sebastiano Paoli, *Codice diplomatico del sacro militare ordine Gerosolimitano oggi di Malta* (Lucca, 1773), 1, p. 6.

to Schlumberger, dates from the early period of Norman rule in Antioch, and therefore cannot be ascribed to Bohemond II. [112] I believe that no one has as yet pointed out the similarities between the obverse of this coin and the seal which Bohemond used as lord of Bari. [113]

The resemblance between the two busts of Peter are very striking, the chief difference being that on the seal Peter is giving the benediction with his left hand and holds the cross in his right, while on the coin the position of the hands is reversed. The difference is to be accounted for by the difference in the iconographical conventions of the West and the Byzantine East.

A copy of Bohemond's seal as prince of Antioch which is still in existence, is of lead, and bears on the obverse around the circumference the legend,:

BOAMUND:PRINCEPS:ANTIOGK: COMES :TRL:,

and the representation of a knight on horseback, bearing a shield pointed at the bottom, and holding in his right hand a banner; he is depicted as turning in the saddle and looking backward. The reverse bears a representation of Saints Peter and Paul, the former holding in his right hand a cross and in his left the keys, while the latter carries a staff and scrip; the reverse also bears the legend:

SANCTVS PETRVS: SANCTVS PAVLVS. [114]

---

112. Gustave Schlumberger, *Numismatique de l'Orient latin* (Paris, 1878), 1, p. 43 and pl. 2, 4.
113. See *supra*, chapter 3.
114. Philippus Paruta and Leonardus Augustinus, *Sicilia numismatica* (Leyden, 1723), 1, cols. 1261-1262; 2, tab. 188, no. 1.

CHAPTER 7

Bohemond in the West, 1105-1107

Bohemond's return to Italy was greeted with the greatest enthusiasm. Kerboga's tent, which he had sent to the Church of St. Nicholas at Bari after the defeat of the Turkish *emir*, [1] had served to keep up the interests of his subjects in his fortunes, and he now brought back with him many other souvenirs and relics; he is said to have given to the Church of St. Sabinus at Canosa what purported to be two thorns from the crown of Christ, still bearing traces of the Redeemer's blood. [2] People flocked to gaze at him, says the author of the *Historia belli sacri*, "as if they were going to see Christ himself." [3]

We know little of Bohemond's activities in the year 1105. He may have visited Pope Paschal II with Daimbert soon after his arrival. [4] Part of his time was devoted to the construction of a fleet for the transport of the armies which he hoped to raise. [5] He also directed legates to Henry I of England, exposing the reasons for his return to the West, and insinuating his desire to visit the English court. Henry, however, fearing that this latest enterprise of the Norman adventurer would draw too many knights from England, discouraged him from making the journey, and suggested that he would meet him in France. [6] The meeting, however, never took place, [7] although Anselm, archbishop of Canterbury, possibly acting as Henry's representative later met Bohe-

1. *Hist. bel. sacr.*, p. 206.

2. Angelus Andreas Tortora, Relatio *status s. primatialis ecclesiae Canusinae sen Historia* (Rome, 1758), p. 180.

3. *Hist. bel. sacr.*, p. 228.

4. *Ibid.*; Bartolf, p. 538.

5. HE, p. 293.

6. Ord., 4, p. 211.

7. Wilhelm Tavernier, *Beiträge zur Rolandsforschung* in *Zeitschrift für französische Sprache und Litteratur*, 1912, 39, Abhandlungen, p. 153, n. 46.

mond in Normandy. [8] Further evidence of Bohemond's attempts to obtain men from England is to be found in the letter written to him in 1106 by Gerald, archbishop of York. [9]

In September, 1105, [10] Bohemond left northern Italy, and went to Rome. The period of his sojourn in that city cannot be determined exactly, but on November 18, Paschal issued a privilege in favour of the Church of St. Nicholas at Bari, at the request of Bohemond. [11] It seems evident that, from the very first, the prince of Antioch had planned to attack Alexius from the West, instead of taking his expedition to the East to be used for the defence of Antioch. His whole itinerary through Italy and France was taken up with attacks upon the Greek emperor, [12] and with exhortations to the fighting-men of the West to join in an expedition against the Empire.

There is no question then of the deflection of the expedition from its original purpose, when Bohemond attacks Durazzo; to attack the Greek Empire from the West was the original purpose of the expedition, and everyone was aware of the fact. The attitude of the West toward Alexius at this period was favourable to Bohemond's undertaking, for it was not uncommonly believed that Alexius had been responsible for the difficulties of the First Crusade, [13] and the disasters of the Crusade of 1101, [14] and that pilgrims from the West to the Holy Land were maltreated on their way through the Greek Empire. [15] Manasses, bishop of Barcelona, who had been commissioned by Alexius to assure the pope of his innocence of the failure of the Crusade of 1101, had done exactly the opposite, and had given reports of the emperor's treachery at the Council of Benevento in 1102.

As a result, according to Albert of Aachen, Paschal had given him letters of authorization and he had visited the nobles of France, preaching of the treachery of the emperor. [16] Paschal II, an enthusiast for the

---

8. Eadmerus, *Historia novorum* in Anglia, edited by Martin Rule (London, 1884), pp. 179-180.

9. *Quadripartitus: Ein englisches Rechtsbuch von* 1114, edited by Felix Liebermann (Halle, 1892), p. 161.

10. *An. Bar. Chron.*, p. 155.

11. Migne, 163, col. 178.

12. Anna, 2, pp. 132, 135, 167-168; Ord., 4, pp. 211-213.

13. WT, pp. 460-461. The *Gesta Francorum* must have done much to prejudice the West against Alexius.

14. HE, pp. 235-237; Alb., p. 584; WT, p. 461.

15. Bernoldus, Chronicon, MGSS, 5, p. 466; *Narratio Floriacensis de captis Antiochia et Hierosolyma et obsesso Dyrrachio, Rec., Hist, occ.*, 5, p. 362; WT, p. 401.

16. Alb., pp. 584-585.

crusading movement, [17] and evidently not averse to seeing it used against the Greek Empire, favoured Bohemond's plans, gave him the banner of St. Peter, [18] and appointed Bruno, bishop of Segni, who had been present with Urban II at the Council of Clermont, [19] as papal legate, with directions to preach the expedition through France, and probably throughout the West in general. [20] Bohemond's expedition against Alexius had ceased to be a mere political movement; it had now received the approval of the Church, and assumed the dignity of a Crusade.

There were two important reasons why Bohemond desired to go to France; first, for the purpose of raising troops for his expedition, and second, in order to contract a marriage with Constance, daughter of Philip of France, and to secure another French princess as a wife for Tancred. It is impossible to determine when Bohemond opened negotiations with the French court in regard to the marriage. Richard of the Principate, who, according to Ordericus Vitalis, was sent by Bohemond to France not long after his release from captivity, [21] may have begun the negotiations. Constance, the daughter of Philip and Bertha of Holland, had been married to Hugh, count of Troyes, but had been divorced from him on the grounds of consanguinity, probably at the end of 1104, or early in 1105. [22] Cecilia, who was secured as a wife for Tancred, was the daughter of Philip by Bertrada de Montfort. [23]

According to Ordericus Vitalis, Bohemond entered France late in February [24] or in March, 1106. [25] His first visit was to the shrine of St. Leonard at Noblac in Limousin, where in fulfilment of the vow which he had made during his captivity, he said his prayers and de-

17. Bernard Monod, *Essai sur les rapports de Pascal II avec Philippe Ier* (1099-1108) (Paris, 1907), pp. 45-46.
18. Bartolfus de Nangeio, p. 538.
19. Bernhard Gigalski, *Bruno, Bischof von Segni, Abt von Monte-Cassino* (1049-1123); *Sein Leben und seine Schriften* (Minister, 1898), p. 58.
20. Suger, p. 22; *Historia peregrinorum*, p. 298; *Chronica monasterii Casinensis*, p. 777.
21. Ord., 4, p. 156.
22. Suger, p. 22; Ivo Carnotensis, *Opera omnia*, Migne, *Pat. lat.*, 162, cols. 163-164; *Historia regum Francorum monasterii sancti Dionysii*, MGSS, 9, p. 405; Hugo Floriacensis, *Liber qui modernorum regum Francorum continet actus*, MGSS, 9; Achille Luchaire, *Louis VI le* Gros; *Annales de sa vie et de son règne* (1081-1137) (Paris, 1890), no. 30, pp. 18-19; Augustin Fliche, *Le règne de Philippe Ier, roi de France* (1060-1108), (Paris, 1912), pp. 87-88; Monod, p. 45.
23. WT, p. 450; *Historia regum Francorum*, p. 405; Anna, 2, p. 132; Wil. Malm., 2, p. 454.
24. Ord., 2, p. 448.
25. *Ibid.*, 4, p. 210.

posited silver fetters as an offering to the saint for his release from Turkish captivity. [26] Sometime after his visit to Noblac, Bohemond had an interview with Philip and completed the arrangement for the marriage. [27]

After leaving his baggage and a part of his train of attendants at Chartres, [28] he travelled throughout France during Lent, greeted with the greatest enthusiasm wherever he went; entertained in monasteries, in castles, and in cities, he told of his adventures in the Orient, and exhibited the relics which he had brought back with him from the Holy Land. [29]

So great was his vogue, that many nobles came to him with their infant sons and asked him to act as godfather to them; the Crusader acquiesced, and the babies received the name of Bohemond. "Hence," says Ordericus, "this celebrated name, which formerly was unusual throughout almost the whole West, was now made common in Gaul."[30] Bohemond took advantage of the great crowds which assembled to see him, and inveighed against the perfidy of Alexius, calling him a pagan and an enemy of the Christians;[31] he undoubtedly made much of the emperor's part in the failure of the Crusade of 1101 and of the molestation of pilgrims passing through the Byzantine Empire. In his train, he had a number of Greek nobles, one of them posing as a son of the emperor, Romanus Diogenes, and pretender to the Greek throne. [32]

Bohemond extended his itinerary at least as far north as Flanders, for on March 30 he was at St. Omer; [33] he probably also accompanied

26. *Ibid.*, pp. 210-212; *Historia peregrinorum*, p. 228; Gaufredus Vosiensis, p. 297; Wil. Malm., 2, p. 454.

27. Ord., 4, p. 213.

28. Eadmerus, p. 180.

29. Ord., 4, p. 212; *Chronicon Vindocinense sen de Aquaria*, in Paul Marchegay and Emile Mabille, Eds., *Chroniques des églises d'Anjou* (Paris, 1869), pp. 171-172.

30. Ord., 4, pp. 212-213. Bohemond seems to have frequently acted as godfather in the Orient also. He stood as sponsor to a Turk who was baptized while the crusading army was at Antioch, and who received the name of Bohemond. Raim., p. 305; Alb., pp. 381-382. He is also said to have sponsored Firuz, who likewise took the name of Bohemond. Guib., p. 212; Baldr. Dol., p. 79, var. 2. It is not improbable that he acted in a similar capacity at the baptism of the commander of the citadel of Antioch. HG, pp. 380-381. Orphaned children on the First Crusade, whose names were unknown, sometimes received the name of Bohemond. Guib., p. 241.

31. Anna, 2, pp. 131-132, 135; Ord., p. 212.

32. Ord., p. 212.

33. Lambertus Audomariensis, *Chronica*, MGSS, 5, p. 66.

Bruno to Mons. [34] Sometime in the second half of April, [35] Bohemond and Bruno arrived at Rouen, where they held a consultation with Anselm, archbishop of Canterbury, and William, archbishop of Rouen, in regard to the Crusade. A certain Ilgyrus, one of the officers in Bohemond's army, who had known Anselm for years, entertained the archbishop with stories of the wars in the East and the geography of the Holy Land, and told him of the relics he had brought back with him and the way in which he had obtained them. He prized above all some of the hair of the Virgin Mary, which had been given to him by the patriarch of Antioch. [36] We do not know how successful Bohemond was in gaining recruits for his army in Normandy; the troubled conditions of the province, due to the quarrel between Henry I of England and Robert, undoubtedly hindered his plans to some extent. [37]

Bohemond's marriage to Constance was celebrated at Chartres, where Adele, the widow of the Crusader, Stephen of Blois, had prepared a great wedding-feast. [38] The exact date of the ceremony cannot be fixed; Ordericus simply says that it took place after Easter, [39] which was on March 25. The marriage took place very probably soon after Bohemond's return from Normandy. A great crowd assembled at Chartres for the wedding, including Philip, his son, Louis the Fat, and the chief prelates and nobles of the realm. [40] After the ceremony had been performed, Bohemond mounted into the organ-loft of the church, and harangued the immense crowd below; he told of his adventures in the East, and urged all the armed men to accompany him in his expedition against Alexius, promising them rich cities and towns as a reward.

Many pressed forward to take the cross, "and took the way to Jerusalem, as if they were hastening to a banquet." [41] The marriage with Constance was a happy stroke of policy on Bohemond's part, for his expedition now had not only the support of the pope, but of Philip of

---

34. Johannes Longus de Ipra, *Chronica monasterii sancti Bertini*, MGSS, 25, p. 787. Bruno's visit is dated incorrectly as having taken place in 1104.

35. For the date, see Tavernier, p. 154, n. 47.

36. Eadmerus, pp. 79-80; *Breve Chronicon Gemmeticense*, in Martin Bouquet, *Recueil des historiens des Gaules et de la France* (Paris, 1838- 1876), 12, p. 775.

37. Gigalski, p. 61.

38 Ord., 2, p. 448, 4, p. 213.

39. *Ibid.*

40. Suger, p. 22.

41. Ord., 4, p. 213.

France, as well. It says much for the reputation which Bohemond had gained for himself in the East, that he, who twenty years before had been a landless noble in southern Italy, now found himself in a position to marry the daughter of the king of France. [42]

It is difficult exactly to determine Bohemond's itinerary, after he left Chartres. On May 17, Bruno was at Le Mons, [43] and later went to St. Lomer, [44] but we do not know whether he was accompanied by Bohemond or not. According to the Angevin chronicles, Bohemond travelled through Anjou after his marriage, and visited Angers, where he was received in all the churches "with great honour and no little reverence." [45] The time is roughly indicated by the earthquake on May 4, which is mentioned directly after the account of Bohemond's visit, as having taken place "in these days." [46] From Angers, Bohemond went to Bourges. [47] On June 26, a council was held at Poitiers, where, in addition to the consideration of other matters, both Bruno and Bohemond made speeches to awaken enthusiasm for the Crusade. [48]

Mansi has conjectured that Poitiers was selected as the place for the council, since it was in the heart of the district which had sent so many men on the ill-fated Crusade of 1101, and hence would be likely to have a strong animus against the emperor. [49] According to Suger, who was present at the council, Bohemond and Bruno gained many recruits by their speeches. [50] From Poitiers, Bohemond, accompanied by Constance and the recruits for his expedition, started for Italy. [51] It is probable that Bohemond did not return home directly, but

---

42. Guib., p. 152: "*Videat qui vult hodie filii ejus Boemundi potentiam, qui, veterem obliterata vilitate parentum, Philippi regis Francorum filiam duxit in conjugium. . . .*" In addition to the sources already quoted, see for the marriage: HF, pp. 482-483; Guib., p. 254; WT, p. 450, Matthieu d'Edesse, pp. 73-74.

43. Gigalski, pp. 61-62.

44. *Ibid.*, p. 63.

45. Rainaldus archidiaconus Andegavensis *Chronica,* Marchegay and Mabille, p. 15; *Chronicae s. Albini Andegavensis,* Marchegay and Mabille, p. 31.

46. Rainaldus, p. 15.

47. *Ibid.*

48. *Chronicon s. Maxentii Pictavensis,* Marchegay and Mabille, p. 423; Suger, p. 23; *Chronicon Kemperlegiense,* Bouquet 12, p. 526; *Chron. Mon. Cas.,* p. 777. According to the *Chronicon sancti Maxentii,* Paschal held a council in Italy, presumably for the same purpose.

49. Mansi, 20, cols. 1205-1207.

50. Suger, p. 23.

51. *Ibid.* The *Historia peregrinorum* says there were one hundred knights in his retinue. *Historia peregrinorum,* p. 229.

probably accompanied Bruno, who journeyed into the south-western part of France; [52] this is confirmed by Ekkehard's statement that Bohemond went as far as Spain. [53] Bruno passed through Toulouse on his way into Italy,[54] and according to Cafaro, Bohemond and Constance visited Genoa on their journey homewards. [55] The Norman prince and his wife reached Apulia in August, [56] and Bohemond resumed his superintendence of the building of a fleet.

In the meantime, Alexius had busied himself in strengthening the defences of his empire against this new menace from the West. Anna implies that her father first heard of Bohemond's arrival in the West through the messages of the Greek governor of Corfu, but this portion of the princess's narrative, containing the story of Bohemond's journey in the coffin and his harangue to the commander of Corfu, is improbable, to say the least. [57]

On learning of Bohemond's plans, Alexius straightway sent messages to Pisa, Genoa and Venice, seeking to persuade them not to join the Norman, [58] and in order to overcome his unpopularity to the west of the Adriatic, he effected the release of three hundred Christian knights, who had been held captive by the *caliph* of Cairo; after being lavishly entertained by Alexius, they returned to the West, in order to contradict Bohemond's malicious attacks upon the emperor.[59] He recalled the troops of Cantacuzenus and Monastras from Cilicia, appointing the Armenian, Oschin, commander of the troops which were left to defend Cilicia against Tancred; [60] he also recruited new troops.[61]

Recognizing that much depended upon the defence of Durazzo, Alexius recalled John, the son of the *sebastocrator* Isaac, and appointed John's brother, Alexius, as governor of the city;[62] at the same time, he gave orders for a fleet to be collected from the Cyclades, and from the sea-coast cities of Europe and Asia, [63] and wrote to Venice for aid

52. Gigalski, p. 66.
53. HE, p. 293.
54. Gigalski, p. 67.
55. Cafarus, *Annales*, p. 15.
56. *An. Bar. Chron.*, p. 155.
57. Anna, 2, pp. 128-132.
58. *Ibid.*, p. 132.
59. *Ibid.*, pp. 133-136. Cf. Ord., 4, pp. 137-138; Alb., p. 649.
60. Anna, 2, p. 136; Chalandon, *Alexis*, p. 239, and n. 1.
61. Anna, 2, p. 148.
62. *Ibid.*
63. *Ibid.*

in the shape of a fleet.[64] A revolt of the Servians,[65] and a conspiracy among some of the great nobles of the Empire to overthrow Alexius,[66] interrupted, no doubt, the preparation for war, but both insurrections were put down effectually by the emperor.

Sometime in 1106, or perhaps early in 1107, Alexius appointed Isaac Contostephanus to the command of the Greek fleet in the Adriatic, with orders to patrol the seas between Apulia and Epirus, and threatened him with the loss of his eyes if he failed to anticipate Bohemond's crossing. Alexius also urged the commander of Durazzo to be on the alert to learn of the enemies' approach. Contostephanus, ignorant of the usual routes which ships took between Italy and Albania, proved an inefficient commander; in violation of his orders, he sailed to the Apulian coast, and prepared to attack Otranto. A ruse, however, of a woman, said to be the mother of Tancred, who was in command of the city, delayed the Greek attack, until one of her sons arrived with reinforcements. After a hard fight, the Greeks were driven into the sea, or back to their boats, and Contostephanus set sail for Avlona. [67] The Normans captured six Petcheneg mercenaries, who were engaged in plundering, and Bohemond, always alive to an opportunity, conducted the barbarian mercenaries, weapons and all, to the pope, and denounced Alexius before the pontiff, for using such savage pagans against Christian adversaries. [68]

Bohemond spent the period from August 1106 to September 1107 in the building of his fleet at Brindisi,[69] while the army of pilgrims and adventurers which had flocked to his standards waited for the expedition to set out, and lived in the meantime on Bohemond's bounty. Although the cost of the food for the army and of the fodder for the horses had almost drained his purse, he nevertheless offered all free transportation in the fleet. At length, in September 1107, all preparations were completed, and the expedition was ready to start.

---

64. Dandulus, col. 261.
65. Anna, 2, p. 149.
66. *Ibid.*, pp. 151-162.
67. *Ibid.*, pp. 165-167, 168-169.
68. *Ibid.*, pp. 167-168.
69. *An. Bar. Chron.*, p. 155; HF, pp. 518-519; Radulphus Tortarius, *Poema de obsidione Dyrrachii*, Cod. Vat. Reg., 1357, f. 126.

CHAPTER 8

The Crusade of 1107

I have already shown above [1] that Bohemond's expedition was a real Crusade; it had received the approval of the pope and was preached by the papal legate, and the usual crusading privileges were given to those who took the cross. [2] In one sense, all of the yearly expeditions to the Holy Land, which took place under the auspices of the Church, were Crusades, even if their comparatively small size has prevented them from being denominated by numbers like the Crusades of 1096 and 1147 and the other great Crusades which succeeded them. If Bruno of Segni was less successful than either Peter of Amiens or Bernard of Clairvaux in inducing men to take the cross, the Crusade which he preached was, nevertheless, in my estimation, of sufficient size to justify our giving it some special denomination and calling it the Crusade of 1107. [3] It is important to note that this expedition is the first example of the use of the Crusade for political purposes; in this sense it is a foreshadowing of the Fourth Crusade. Paschal's part in the movement throws an interesting light upon papal policy in its dealings with the Byzantine Empire. [4]

In September 1107 Bohemond heard mass in the Church of St. Nicholas at Bari, and collecting his forces, which seem to have been encamped at this city, [5] marched to Brindisi, whence he set sail on October 9 for the Albanian coast. [6] According to the anonymous Chroni-

1. See *supra*, chapter 7.
2. For the complications arising from the privileges of Hugh of Puiset, a leader in Bohemond's army, see Ivo Carnotensis, 2, cols. 170-172.
3. Ordericus refers to Bohemond's expedition as "*tertia profectio Occidentalium* in Jerusalem," Ord., 4, pp. 448-49.
4. For Paschal's policy, see Norden, pp. 71-73.
5. *An. Bar. Chron.*, p. 155; *Narratio Floriacensis*, p. 361; Radulphus Tortarius, f. 126.
6. HF, pp. 519-520; *An. Bar. Chron.* gives the date, October 10, (continued next page.)

cle of Bari, there were two hundred large and small ships in the fleet, in addition to thirty galleys; the army, foot and horse, was estimated at 34,000 men.[7] Fulk places the number at five thousand horsemen, and sixty thousand foot-soldiers,[8] Albert at twelve thousand horsemen and sixty thousand foot-soldiers,[9] William of Tyre at five thousand horse and forty thousand foot.[10] Anna gives no definite figures for the size of Bohemond's army, but says that twelve large ships, furnished with double banks of oars, formed the nucleus of the fleet.[11] Ralph Tortaire says that the number of troops was infinite, "like the birds of the spring or the sands of the sea," and places the number of ships at four thousand, a quite ridiculous figure.[12] The estimates of the Chronicle of Bari probably approximate most closely to the truth.

Bohemond's troops were probably drawn, for the most part, from France and Italy,[13] although Anna claims that there were also English, Germans, and Spaniards in his army;[14] according to the Narrative of Fleury, troops were recruited not only from France, but from all parts of the West as well.[15] Ralph Tortaire gives a list of doubtful value of the districts and cities which furnished troops; it is interesting to note that he mentions Pisa and Genoa.[16] It is very likely that these cities, in view of their relations with Antioch, contributed to the expedition in the shape of maritime aid. The Crusade of 1107 was primarily a military expedition, and unlike the earlier Crusades, included no women or children in its ranks.[17]

Among the leaders of the expedition were Guy, Bohemond's half-brother, who had been appointed to act as second-in-command,[18] Hugh of Puiset, viscount of Chartres, who later succeeded to Guy's position.[19] Ralph the Red of Pont-Echanfré, and his brother Joscel-

but this probably applies to the day of landing in Greece. Anna errs in making Bari the port of departure. Anna, 2, p. 172.

7. *An. Bar. Chron.*, p. 155.

8. HF, p. 521.

9. Alb., p. 650.

10. WT, p. 461.

11. Anna, 2, pp. 170-171.

12. Radulphus Tortarius, f. 126.

13. Alb., p. 650.

14. Anna, 2, p. 172.

15. *Narratio Floriacensis*, p. 361

16. Radulphus Tortarius, ff. 125-126.

17. HF, p. 521.

18. Radulphus Tortarius, f. 127.

19. *Ibid.*, 131.

lin, Simon of Anet, Robert of Maule, Hugh Sans-Avoir, [20] William Claret,[21] Robert de Montfort, who had been condemned by Henry I of England for violation of faith, [22] Rainer the Brown, Philip of Mont d'Or, and Robert of Vieuxpont-sur-Dive. [23]

Contostephanus, in the meanwhile, conjecturing that Bohemond would attempt to land at Avlona, recalled his large ships which were scattered along the coast from Durazzo to Chimara, and stationed lookouts on the Hill of Jason. On learning from a Frank, probably a deserter, that Bohemond was about to cross, Contostephanus feigned illness, gave up his office, and retired to take the baths at Chimara, while Landulf, ablest by far of the Greek naval commanders, succeeded to the command of the Adriatic fleet. [24]

With the advantage of a favouring wind, the Norman fleet crossed the Adriatic in safety and approached the Albanian coast. Landulf, recognizing the inferiority of his own squadron, made no attempt to intercept the great Norman fleet, and allowed it to occupy Avlona, without striking a blow, on October 10, 1107. [25] The army then disembarked, and went into camp. [26] During the following days, Bohemond's troops occupied Canina, [27] and ravaged the town and country districts of Epirus, [28] and on October 13, they appeared before Durazzo and laid siege to "the western gate of the Empire." [29]

The governor of Durazzo, as soon as he had learned that Bohemond had landed, dispatched a fleet Scythian messenger to Constantinople with the news. The courier, coming upon the emperor as he was returning from the hunt, prostrated himself before him, and cried out in a loud voice that Bohemond had landed. The dread name of the Norman transfixed everyone with fear, except the emperor, who began to unlace his boots, and said quietly, "Let us dine now; we shall see about Bohemond afterwards." [30]

---

20. Ord., 4, pp. 213, 239.

21. Alb., p. 651; Anna, 2, p. 215.

22. Ord., 4, pp. 239-240.

23. *Narratio Floriacensis*, p. 361. The poem of Ralph Tortaire contains a number of names which may or may not be authentic.

24. Anna, 2, pp. 169-170.

25. *An. Bar. Chron.*, p. 155; Anna, 2, pp. 171-172; HF, p. 520; Alb., p. 560.

26. Radulphus Tortarius, f. 126.

27. *An. Bar. Chron.*, p. 155.

28. Anna, 2, p. 172; *Narratio Floriacensis*, p. 361; WT, p. 461; Alb., p. 650; Radulphus Tortarius, f. 126.

29. HF, p. 520; Anna, 2, p. 172; *Narratio Floriacensis*, p. 361; Alb., p. 650.

30. Anna, 2, pp. 174-175.

Thus far, Bohemond's campaign had proceeded on lines similar to that of his father's campaign of 1081, but he was destined to be less successful at Durazzo. Failing to take the city by a sudden attack,[31] and finding that it was strongly defended and well provisioned, he pitched his camp to the east of Durazzo, and spent the winter in laying plans and in building siege- machines, while his troops occupied Petrula and Mylus, on the other side of the Deabolis.[32]

In the meanwhile, the Greek fleets, which had been augmented in December by a Venetian fleet under Ordelafus Faletro,[33] cut off Bohemond's communication with Italy, and prevented reinforcements from reaching him, while the Greek troops held the mountain-passes about Durazzo, and prevented the Crusaders from wandering far afield in search of food. As a result, after the environs of Durazzo had been devastated, the Franks began to feel the perils of hunger. Men and horses perished during the famine, and an intestinal disease, induced by the consumption of spoiled grain, carried off many more.[34] Alexius left Constantinople in November, and spent the winter at Salonika, drilling his army.[35]

In the spring of 1108, Bohemond burned his transports,[36] as his father had done in 1081, and began to push the siege more vigorously. A great battering-ram, protected by a *testudo*, which was covered by ox-hides and mounted on wheels, was brought up to the eastern wall and swung against it. Some impression was made on the fortifications, but the defenders of the city, jeering at the efforts of the Crusaders, opened their gates and mockingly invited them to enter. Seeing that they could do little by making a breach in the walls, Bohemond's men ceased their efforts, and left the machine, which had been rendered stationary by the removal of its wheels, to be burned by the Greeks. An attempt to undermine the walls of the city by tunnelling through the hill on which the northern section of Durazzo was built was foiled by a Greek counter-mine, and the excavators were driven from their tunnel by having a form of Greek fire shot into their faces.

Bohemond now brought up the most formidable of his machines, a great wooden tower, which had been under construction almost

---

31. Anna, 2, p. 184.
32. HF, p. 521.
33. *Annales Venetici breves*, MGSS, 14, p. 70; Dandulus, col. 261.
34 Anna, 2, pp. 178, 184-186.
35. *Ibid.*, pp. 182-183.
36. *Ibid.*, p. 184.

since the beginning of the siege. The height of the city walls had been estimated with a great nicety, and the tower was built so as to top them by five or six cubits. It was equipped with drawbridges which could be let down upon the walls, had several stories, and was pierced with windows at frequent intervals, from which missiles could be cast; the whole machine was mounted on wheels, and was propelled by soldiers hidden inside the base, so that when it was in motion, it appeared like a great giant, advancing by its own power.

On beholding this terrible machine approaching the walls, Alexius, the governor of Durazzo, ordered the construction of a lofty scaffolding on the walls, opposite the tower, and surpassing it in height by a cubit. From this the Greek soldiers launched their liquid fire at the tower, but finding that it did not take effect, they filled up the space between the walls and the tower with inflammable material well soaked with oil, and then ignited the mass with their Greek fire. The tower, which had been rendered immovable by the removal of the wheels, was soon in flames, and the soldiers in it were consumed by the flames or were forced to fling themselves to the ground. The glare of the conflagration could be seen for a long distance about the besieged city, and a great cry which went up from Bohemond's troops bore witness to their dismay at the destruction of their mightiest machine. [37]

In the spring, Alexius arrived in Albania, and went into camp at Deabolis. [38] Anna does not indicate the size of her fathers' army, but the author of the *Narrative of Fleury* puts it at the exaggerated figure of sixty thousand; [39] it was a typical motley Byzantine army, including in its ranks Greeks, Turks, [40] Cumani, Petchenegs, [41] and Alans. [42] Alexius had profited by the mistakes of which he had been guilty in the campaign of 1081, and now decided not to risk a great battle with Bohemond, but to guard the mountain passes with his troops and the coasts with his fleet, in the hopes that the rigid blockade would force the Norman to come to terms. He stationed his most trusted troops

37. Anna, 2, pp. 186-193; Alb., p. 650.
38. Anna, 2, p. 193. Alb., pp. 650-651, places the camp at Batolia, a day's journey from Durazzo.
39. *Narratio Floriacensis*, p. 361.
40. Anna, 2, p. 204; Alb., p. 651; Radulphus Tortarius, f. 127. According to Ibn el-Athîr, p. 242, Alexius solicited and received aid from Kilij Arslan.
41. Alb., p. 651. Radulphus Tortarius, ff. 126-127, gives a fanciful list of the people in the Greek army.
42. Anna, 2, p. 204.

in the important defiles to prevent all traitorous communication between his army and Bohemond's. Avoiding a decision by arms, he had recourse to the subtler weapons of Greek guile.

Summoning Marinus Sebastus, the Neapolitan, a certain Roger, and Peter of Aulps, all Westerners in his service, he inquired and learned from them the names of Bohemond's most trusted commanders. According to Anna, he then wrote a number of letters to Bohemond's brother, Guy, the count of Conversano, a certain Richard, Richard of the Principate, and several other leaders, purporting to be the answers to letters of a treasonable nature which they had sent to him. Hoping that these letters, when they came into Bohemond's hands would drive him to some rash move and spread dissension in the besieging army, Alexius ordered his messengers to deliver them to the Norman leaders, while he sent one of his trusted subjects ahead, with instructions to pose as a deserter and to pretend to betray the emissaries with their messages into Bohemond's hands.

The ruse succeeded, the messengers were captured, and Bohemond read the letters. Instead of giving command for the immediate arrest of the suspected commanders, however, he shut himself up in his tent for six days, and after much deliberation, seems to have concluded that the letters had been written to mislead him, and thereafter took no further steps in the matter. [43]

The Western sources, on the other hand, are convinced of the fact that Bohemond's officers betrayed him to the emperor. According to Ordericus Vitalis, Guy and Robert de Montfort, won over by Alexius' gifts, did all in their power to make Bohemond's attacks a failure and to forewarn the Greeks of his plans; Guy died soon after the close of the war, without receiving his brother's pardon. [44] According to the *Narrative* of Fleury, Guy confessed to Bohemond on his deathbed that Alexius had promised him his daughter in marriage, together with Durazzo and other gifts, and that he himself had frequently dissuaded the inhabitants of Durazzo from surrendering when they were on the point of doing so. Bohemond not only refused to pardon his erring brother, but cursed him before he died. [45]

Albert of Aachen refers to the treason of Guy, whom he makes Bohemond's nephew, of William Claret, and of the other leaders. [46]

---

43. Anna, 2, pp. 195-199.
44. Ord., 4, pp. 240-241, 243.
45. *Narratio Floriacensis*, p. 362.
46. Alb., p. 651.

William of Malmesbury likewise speaks of treason on the part of Bo-hemond's officers. [47] In spite of the agreement of the sources just cited, I am of the opinion that they are in error, and that Anna Comnena is right in making no mention of the fact that the Norman command-ers were tampered with by Alexius. The Western authorities were not present on the campaign, and do not seem to have been very well informed regarding it. Anna, on the other hand, was in a position to know if there had been negotiations between her father and the offic-ers of the Norman army.

One might ask why, if Guy and the others were guilty of treason, Anna, who is always only too willing to prove the Franks guilty of avarice and duplicity, should have taken pains to conceal the fact. I do not doubt that there was talk of treachery among the rank and file of the army after Bohemond had been forced to make peace, for it must have been difficult to explain why their commander should have given up the campaign without having encountered the Greeks in a single decisive battle, but outside of the desertion of William Claret and other minor leaders, I see no reason for doubting the good faith of Guy and his comrades.

In the meanwhile, Alexius had garrisoned all the mountain passes and barricaded all the roads about Durazzo, and, in addition, seems to have recovered some of the places which had been occupied by the Normans, for we find him appointing Michael Cecaumenus com-mander of Aulon, Hiericho, and Canina, Alexander Cabasilas of Petru-la, Leo Nicerita of Deura, and Eustathius Camytzes of Arbanum. [48]

Bohemond dispatched a body of troops under Guy against Petrula, but learning about the roads near Arbanum from the inhabitants of some small towns in the vicinity which had come into Bohemond's power, Guy changed his plans and decided to attack Camytzes at Ar-banum. Two of his officers, Count Saracen and Count Pagan with their troops were guided around to Camytzes' rear by people from Deura, while Guy himself advanced from the front. Camytzes' army was caught between the two Norman forces, and crushingly defeat-ed. [49]

The *Narrative of Fleury* contains the description of a battle fought between a crusading force under Hugh of Puiset, Rainer the Brown, Philip of Mont d'Or, and Robert of Vieuxpont and a Greek army

---

47. Wil. Malm., 2, pp. 401, 454.
48. Anna, 2, p. 199.
49. *Ibid.*, pp. 199-200; Alb., p. 651.

on Easter Sunday, April 5, at the foot of a mountain, on which was a certain "*castrum Corbianum*." The battle raged from the third hour till evening, and the Greeks were so signally defeated that hardly one escaped to bear the news of the disaster. [50] Wilken has wished to identify this battle with the defeat of Camytzes, [51] although, to speak frankly, there is practically no similarity in the accounts of the two engagements. The *Narrative of Fleury* then adds that the expedition on its way back to Durazzo attacked and routed another Greek force near a place called the "Ladder of Saint George."

As the result of the defeat and death of Alyates at Glabinitza during the winter, [52] Alexius summoned Cantacuzenus from Laodicea, and placed him in charge of an expedition against Glabinitza. After holding a council of war at Petra, Alexius returned to Deabolis, while Cantacuzenus went on towards Glabinitza. Marching on the fortress of Mylum, he laid siege to it, and was on the point of taking it, when his scouts announced the approach of a band of Franks who had been on guard on the other side of the River Buse. Cantacuzenus succeeded in delaying his men from flight only long enough to allow him to burn his siege-machines and boats; he then took up his position in a plain with the Charzon River on his right and a marsh on his left. [53]

Guy, learning of Cantacuzenus' activities, sent a portion of his forces against Hiericho and Canina; they defeated Michael Cecaumenus, and rejoined Guy, who now marched against Cantacuzenus. Finding the Greeks occupying a very strong position, Guy avoided a battle, but Cantacuzenus, crossing the river during the night, forced him to fight on the next day. Cantacuzenus himself held the centre, the Turks the left, and the Alans the right, while the Petchenegs were sent ahead as skirmishers, but soon found it necessary to fall back before the attacks of the Prankish cavalry. The Crusaders checked the charges of the Turks and Alans, but finally broke under the attack of the Greeks, and fled in disorder, pursued by the imperial forces as far as Mylum. Many of the Franks were killed, and a number of them were taken prisoners, including a certain Hugh, his brother Richard, and Count Pagan. [54]

50. *Narratio Floriacensis,* p. 361.
51. Friedrich Wilken, *Geschichte der Kreuzzüge* (Leipzig, 1807-1832), 2, p. 344, n. 52.
52. Anna, 2, pp. 200-201. Anna describes the defeat of Alyates immediately after that of Camytzes, but the fact that Cantacuzenus was recalled to Europe from Laodicea as a result of it has led me to place it in the winter or early spring of 1108.
53. Anna, 2, pp. 201-203; Wilken, 2, p. 344, n. 52, has identified this engagement with the battle at the Ladder of St. George.
54. Anna, 2, pp. 203-206.

Bohemond, hemmed in by land and sea, and running short of supplies, sent a force to raid the districts about Avlona, Hiericho and Canina, but a Greek army under Beroites, sent by Cantacuzenus, routed the Crusaders.

Another force of six thousand men which Bohemond sent against Cantacuzenus was attacked by the Greek general early one morning on the banks of the Buse; many of the Crusaders were killed or captured and the rest were put to flight. [55] Cantacuzenus, sending his captives to the emperor, moved on to Timorum, where he attacked and captured a force of one hundred knights from Bohemond's army. Among the captives was a relative of Bohemond, a giant in stature, whose height Anna places at ten feet; he was sent to Alexius under the guard of a very short Petcheneg, and the sight of the giant Norman and his diminutive captor provoked the laughter of all who beheld them. [56]

If Alexius' plans were developing successfully on land, the conduct of the fleet was by no means satisfactory. The emperor was informed through dispatches from Landulf of the gross inefficiency of Isaac and Stephen Contostephanus and Alexander Euphorbenus, who, neglecting their task of patrolling the waters between Italy and Albania, had landed on the Greek coast for recreation. Landulf further complained that Isaac had allowed ships from Italy to take advantage of a favourable wind from the southwest and gain Avlona, while he, unable to sail against the wind, had been compelled to look helplessly on; as a result, Bohemond had received valuable reinforcements of men and supplies. Alexius thereupon wrote to Contostephanus, spurring him on to renewed efforts against the enemies' marine, but the admiral, taking up his position in the middle of the Adriatic, was still unable to deal with the Norman fleets, when they came down on him with the wind.

Alexius then sent him a chart of the Adriatic, on which the main ports of Italy and Illyria and the places where he might station his ships to the best advantage, were indicated. Thereafter Contostephanus had better fortune, and succeeded in burning some ships of the Norman fleet and in sinking others. Before, however, he had heard of Isaac's results, Alexius recalled Marianus Maurocatacalo from the command of Petrula, and placed him in charge of the Adriatic fleet. The appointment was a wise one, and Alexius soon had the satisfaction of seeing all communication between the Norman army and Italy cut

55. *Ibid.*, pp. 206-207; Alb., p. 651.
56. Anna, 2, pp. 207-208.

124

off by the Greek fleet. [57]

The emperor now sent instructions from his headquarters at Deabolis to the commanders of his troops, ordering them to harass the Crusaders, and especially to attempt to shoot down the horses of the knights, for, burdened as they were with their heavy armour, the fall of their horses rendered them helpless, and they could easily be taken prisoners. [58] Meanwhile, Alexius' blockade was causing great suffering in the Crusaders' camp. No supplies could be introduced from Italy, the Crusaders did not dare to go far from camp for food in fear of being cut off by the Greeks, and famine, the heat, and the plague worked havoc in the invaders' ranks. Had Bohemond been able to come into contact with the natives of the hinterland, he would undoubtedly have been able to cause an uprising which would have jeopardized the safety of Alexius' cause, for the emperor was not even sure of a number of his own troops; but the wily Comnenus had control of the roads and his most faithful troops held the passes leading to the interior. [59] As a result of their desperate plight, many of the Crusaders began to steal off in small bands and deserted to the emperor, who, after presenting them with gifts, allowed them to go their way. [60] William Claret, one of Bohemond commanders, deserted to the imperial forces, and informed Alexius of conditions in Bohemond's camp; he was rewarded with many gifts and the title of *nobilissimus*. [61]

Moved by the advice of his officers [62] and the desperate condition of his army, and realizing that he was neither able to capture Durazzo, nor to advance into the interior of Albania, Bohemond decided to seek terms from the Greeks, and opened negotiations with the duke of Durazzo. The emperor was informed by his nephew of Bohemond's step; fearing a conspiracy among his own subjects, and anxious to make peace with Bohemond in order that he might be able to turn his attention to domestic affairs, he sent a message to the prince of Antioch through the duke of Durazzo, reproaching him for his faithlessness, but offering to make peace, and suggesting a conference. On receiving the message, Bohemond refused to go to meet the emperor, unless he received a number of important dignitaries as hostages for

57. Anna, 2, pp. 209-212.
58. *Ibid.*, pp. 212-214.
59. Anna, 2, pp. 214-215; Alb., pp. 651-652; Ord., 4, p. 241; Lisiardus Turonensis, *Secunda pars historiae Iherosolymitanae*, in *Rec., Hist, occ.*, 3, p. 568.
60. Ord., p. 241; Alb., p. 652.
61. Anna, 2, p. 215.
62. Ord., 4, pp. 241-242; *Narratio Floriacensis*, p. 362; Alb., p. 652.

his safety. Alexius therefore sent Marinus the Neapolitan, Roger the Frank, Constantinus Euphorbenus and Adralestus, an interpreter, to confer with the Norman and to act as hostages. Bohemond, unwilling that they should see the miserable condition of his army, met them at some distance from his camp.

They began the conference by assuring him that the emperor had not forgotten the fact that he had violated the oath which he had taken to him in 1097, but were interrupted by Bohemond, who exclaimed, "Enough of such words! If you have anything from the emperor to communicate to me, I wish to hear it." The envoys then revealed Alexius' immediate terms: he asked that Bohemond come to confer with him on the terms of peace, pledging his safe return in case they could not agree, and promising that those of the Crusaders who wished to go on to Jerusalem would be aided by him, while those who wished to return home would receive gifts from him and be allowed to depart.

Bohemond accepted the terms, but demanded that he be received with fitting ceremony by the emperor; he asked that a number of the emperor's closest relations advance more than six stades to meet him as he rode towards Alexius' camp, that when he should enter Alexius' tent, the latter rise from his throne and receive him with due honour, that there be no mention made of the agreement of 1097, that he be allowed to speak his mind freely, that he be allowed to enter the tent with two knights and without bowing his knee or neck, and that the emperor take him by the hand and allow him to stand at the head of his couch. The .Greek envoys rejected the demands that the emperor rise at his entrance and that he be allowed to greet the emperor without bending knee or neck; they granted his other requests, with the stipulation that the personages who met him were to be some of the emperor's more remote relations. The legates then departed for the quarters which had been prepared for them, where they spent the night under guard, lest they should wander about and spy out conditions in the crusading army.

On the morrow, Bohemond rode out to meet them with a train of three hundred knights, but dismissing most of them, he advanced to the conference accompanied by only six. He refused to accept the Greek terms until a certain Hugh in his suite, probably Hugh of Puiset, complained that none of the knights who had followed him against the emperor had had any opportunity for battle, and asserted that it was time to make peace. The prince thereupon agreed to the envoy's terms, but demanded that they swear that he would be allowed to return safely from the emperor's camp. They did so, and he in turn swore that their lives would be safe if he returned unharmed from Deabolis. Marinus Adralestus, and Roger were then handed over to Guy to guard as hostages. [63]

Before he departed for the conference with Alexius, Bohemond asked and received permission to move his camp to a more healthful spot, on condition that he did not move it more than twelve stades. The Greek legates examined the new location of the camp, and sent word to the Greek outposts not to attack the crusading forces. Euphorbenus then received permission from Bohemond to visit Durazzo, where he learned from the duke, Alexius, that all was going well, and that Bohemond's attacks had made no impression on the city's defences. [64]

Euphorbenus, accompanied by Bohemond, then left for the emperor's camp, after sending Manuel Modenus ahead to announce their approach. The emperor extended his hand to Bohemond on his arrival and allowed him to stand at the head of his couch. Alexius began the conference by reviewing past events, but was interrupted by Bohemond who declared that he had not come to answer to charges, and that he had many things to say himself, but that in the future he would allow all such things to the emperor. Alexius then demanded that Bohemond recognize his *suzerainty* and that he force Tancred to do the same, that he hand over Antioch in accordance with the agreement of 1097, and that in the future, he observe all the other terms of the treaty. Bohemond rejected the demand, and asked to be allowed to return to his own camp.

The emperor consented, and proposed to conduct him to Durazzo himself, and gave orders for horses to be made ready. The prince of Antioch retired to the tent which had been prepared for him, and asked for Nicephorus Bryennius, husband of Anna Comnena. Bryennius came, and finally persuaded him to accept Alexius' terms. The treaty was drawn up on the following day (September 1108). [65]

---

63. Anna, 2, pp. 215-222. Radulphus Tortarius, f. 132, makes Bohemond's offer of peace the result of a Pyrrhic victory over the Greeks. The *Narrative of Fleury* says that Alexius made peace, when he realized that the Crusaders could not be overcome. *Narratio Floriacensis*, p. 362. The Western writers, with a few exceptions, tend to minimize Bohemond's defeat.

64. Anna, 2, pp. 222-223.

65. Anna, 2, pp. 224, 226-227. The *Narrative of Fleury* is in error in making Alexius come from Constantinople on a fifteen days' march to (continued next page.)

The agreement between Alexius and Bohemond was incorporated in two documents, one of which was signed by Bohemond and given to Alexius, while the other, a *chrysobull*, was drawn up by Alexius and handed over to Bohemond. The former document, which contains a statement of Bohemond's obligations towards the emperor, has been preserved in Anna's history; the *chrysobull*, which enumerated Alexius' grants and concessions, to Bohemond has been lost, but a portion of its contents can be reconstructed from the text of the documents quoted by Anna, from Anna's own account, and from the remarks of the Western sources. [66]

Bohemond's document, as found in Anna, is really composed of an original draft, and an appendix, which was added at the request of Bohemond and the other Crusaders. [67] The prince of Antioch begins the document, which is couched in the most obsequious terms, with the agreement to consider the pact of 1097 as null and void. He next promises to consider himself the *vassal* of Alexius and his son, John; to take up arms against the emperor's enemies and to come to his aid with all his troops and in person, if he is in a position to do so; to retain no lands which belong to the Empire, except those which are granted him by the emperor; to hand over lands, formerly belonging to the Empire, which have been conquered by him, unless he is allowed by the emperor to keep them.

He agrees not to enter into an alliance detrimental to the emperor's interests, nor to become the *vassal* of any other lord without the emperor's consent, nor to receive fugitive subjects of the emperor who take refuge with him, but to force them by arms to return to the emperor's allegiance. Those lands, which have never been a part of the Empire, and which Bohemond gains in any manner, are to be held as if they have been granted to him by the emperor; new *vassals* are to be recognized only with the emperor's consent, and on condition that they own themselves as *vassals* of the emperor. He engages himself to force his own *vassals* holding lands granted by the emperor to become the *vassals* of the emperor; those with him on the expedition are not to be allowed to return to Italy until they have taken the required

---

meet Bohemond. *Narratio Floriacensis*, p. 362. Zonaras is also incorrect in placing the meeting at Colonia Europaea. Johannes Zonaras, *Epitome historiarum*, edited by L. Dindorf (Leipzig, 1868-1875), 4, p. 246.
66. Anna, 2, pp. 229-230. See Carl Neumann, *Über die urkundlichen Quellen zur Geschichte der bysantinisch-venetianischen Beziehungen vornehmlich im Zeitalter der Komnenen*, in *Byzantinische Zeitschrift*, 1892, 1, pp. 371-372.
67. Anna, 2, p. 242.

oath, while his *vassals* in the East are to take the oath before an imperial official, sent thither for that purpose.

He promises to make war on Tancred unless he gives up all lands, except those expressly granted by Alexius in the *chrysobull*. He is to force the inhabitants of the lands which have been granted to him to take the oath of allegiance to the emperor; they have the right, in case of treason on Bohemond's part toward the emperor, of throwing off their allegiance to him. He will not molest the Saracens who wish to become subjects of the Empire, except those, who, already defeated by his troops, seek safety by claiming protection from the emperor. There is to be no Latin patriarch of Antioch, but the emperor is to appoint a Greek patriarch.

The following cities and districts are granted to Bohemond: Antioch and the lands about it, the Port of St. Simeon, Dux and its lands, Lulus, the Admirable Mountain, Pheresia and its lands, St. Elias and the surrounding towns, Borze and its surrounding towns, the district about Shaizar, Artah, Teluch and its lands, Germanicaea and its towns, Mount Maurus with its fortresses and the adjacent plain with the exception of the lands of the Armenian rulers, Leo and Theodore, who are subjects of the Empire, the districts of Baghras and Palatza, and the theme of Zume. [68] These lands are to be held by Bohemond during his lifetime; he is to have the usufruct of them, but at his death, they are to return to the Empire. A certain number of very important districts and cities are divorced from Antioch: the theme of Podandum, Tarsus, Adana, Mamistra, and Ainzarba, that is, all Cilicia from the Cydnus to the Hermon, Laodicea, Jabala, Valania, Maraclea, and Tortosa.

The appendix to the document, which was added as a result of the pleas of Bohemond and the other Crusaders makes some additions to, and changes in the content of the main body of the document. In return for the lands which were separated from Antioch, Bohemond is to receive the theme of Casiotis, that is, the lands of Aleppo, the theme of Lapara and its towns; Plasta, Chonius, Romaina, Aramisus, Amera, Sarbanus, Telchampson, the three Trilia, including Sthlabotilin, Sgenin, Caltzierin, Commermoeri, Cathismatin, Sarsapen, and Necran; themes about Edessa, the theme of Limnia, and the theme of Actus.

In addition, Alexius is to make him a yearly grant of two hundred pounds in Michaels. Instead of merely holding his eastern lands as a usufruct, as is stipulated in the main body of the document, Bohe-

---

68. For attempts to identify some of the more obscure places mentioned in the document, see Röhricht, Königreich, p. 63, nn. 1, 2, 3; Chalandon, *Alexis*, pp. 247-248.

mond is to hold them as fiefs, with the right of appointing his successor. [69]

The document closes with Bohemond's solemn oath on the cross, the crown of thorns, the nails, and the lance of Christ, that he will fulfil the provisions of the agreement, and was witnessed by Maur, bishop of Amalfi, who had come as papal legate to Alexius, Renard, bishop of Taranto, other Italian clerics, a number of the crusading leaders, and twelve imperial dignitaries and officials, for the most part western in origin. [70]

Fulk of Chartres, [71] and the *Narrative of Fleury* [72] mention Bohemond's oath of homage to the emperor, but conceal or fail to note the degree of his humiliation.

The *chrysobull*, which Bohemond received from Alexius, contained an enumeration of the grants to the Norman, and the concessions of the emperor. We know the lands which were granted to him from the text of the document which we have just examined. Alexius further agreed to guarantee the safety of pilgrims and Crusaders passing through his dominions, [73] a concession which Bohemond must have insisted on, for the mistreatment of pilgrims by the Greeks had been the ostensible cause of his expedition against Alexius. [74] The emperor also conferred upon the defeated prince of Antioch the title of *sebastus*.[75] Whether or not the *chrysobull* contained a statement of the emperor's promise to allow those in Bohemond's expedition who wished to go on to Jerusalem to remain in the Empire during the winter and those who wished to return home to go without molestation, it is impossible to say. [76] The *Narrative of Fleury* contains a statement of Alexius' terms which, for the most part, it is impossible to control or evaluate. The emperor promises that pilgrims passing through

---

69. There is a *lacuna* in the manuscript of the postscript after the words, "καὶ τὰ δουκᾶτον". Reifferscheid, p. 243, n. 10, has suggested "τῆς Ἐδέσσης" as the missing words, thus making it appear that the right of Bohemond to appoint a successor was to be applied to Edessa alone. I believe that Reifferscheid's interpolation is incorrect, since Edessa was not considered as a duchy in the Byzantine administration. I believe that the missing words were probably "τῆς Ἀντιοχείας."

70. Anna, 2, pp. 228-246.

71. HF, p. 524.

72. *Narratio Floriacensis*, p. 362.

73. HF, p. 524; *Narratio Floriacensis*, p. 362; *Historia peregrinorum*, p. 229; Alb., p. 652.

74. Ibid., HF p. 521; *Narratio Floriacensis*, p. 361; Wil. Malm., 2, p. 454.

75. Anna, 2, p. 248.

76. Anna, 2, p. 219; Alb., p. 652.

his dominions will not be injured; any pilgrim, who can prove that violence has been done him, will receive compensation; everyone in Bohemond's army will receive indemnification for the losses which he has sustained; and the emperor will furnish Bohemond with troops to aid him in conquering in Asia Minor an amount of land, whose length and breadth are each to be the distance which can be covered in a fifteen days' journey. [77]

Bohemond, after receiving valuable gifts from Alexius, [78] returned to his camp, accompanied by Constantinus Euphorbenus, and after handing over his army to the Greek commissioners, he sailed for Otranto (September 1108). [79] According to Albert, the Crusaders were much cast down by the fact that Bohemond had stolen away to Apulia, and had failed to remunerate them for the labours they had performed. [80] A portion of the army, unable to afford the expenses of the journey to the Holy Land after the long sojourn at Durazzo, returned home, while the larger part went on to Jerusalem, after spending the winter in the Empire. [81] Bohemond's brother, Guy, died either shortly before or after the end of the expedition. [82]

Bohemond had sustained a crushing defeat, and his designs had gone hopelessly astray, but if he had lost much through his failure at

---

77. *Narratio Floriacensis*, p. 362; The *Narrative* mentions the twelve Greek witnesses whom *Anna enumerates. Cf. Radulphus Tortarius, f. 132.*

Horrida brumali Romani frigore Thurcis
Subdita iam pridem cessit habenda duci;
Quae pars Vulgariae victoris cesserat irae,
Hec eadem solvit iussa tributa sibi;
Quicquid et Ansoniis adquiri quiverit armis.
Aequa lance duum iuris erit procerum,
Induperatorum possessio namque priorum
Extitit Esi fertile clima soli.
Corruet in castris si miles sidere quovis,
Sancius in bello si merit gladio,
Instaurat validas Grecus locuplecior alas;
Aruna ministrabit, subpeditabet equos.

78. Alb., p. 652; *Historia peregrinorum*, p. 229. According to the latter source, Alexius adopted Bohemond as his son.

79. Anna, 2, p. 248. The *Bari Chronicle* places Bohemond's return in October, but in September he made a grant to the Monastery of St. Stephen near Monopoli, seemingly at Bari. *An. Bar. Chron.*, p. 155; *Cod. dip. Bar.*, 2, pp. 221-222.

80. Alb., p. 652; Cf . Ord., 4, p. 242.

81. Anna, 2, p. 248; HF, p. 525; Ord., 4, p. 242; *Historia peregrinorum*, p. 229; *Narratio Floriacensis*, p. 362.

82. *Ibid.*, Ord., 4, p. 243; Lisiardus, p. 568.

Durazzo, Alexius had gained little, for Tancred still ruled undisturbed at Antioch, and successfully extended the boundaries of his uncle's principality in all directions. The treaty of 1108 must have gratified the emperor's *amour propre*, but it brought him nothing tangible.

Little is known of Bohemond's life, after his return from Durazzo. Constance bore him two sons; the elder, John, died in infancy, while the second son, Bohemond, born about 1109,[83] lived to succeed his father as prince of Antioch.[84]

Bohemond's documents for the period after his return from Antioch are neither numerous nor of any great importance. In July, 1107, Geoffrey of Gallipoli, *catapan* of Bari and Giovenazzo, by the favour of Bohemond, prince of Antioch, makes a grant of privileges to the Abbey of Conversano.[85] In the same month, the same official confirmed a donation made by Duke Roger in favour of Grifo, the judge.[86] In the same year, Bohemond granted to the monks of Blessed Lawrence of Aversa exemption from tolls throughout his dominions.[87] In May[88] and June[89] 1108 Bohemond's *catapan* issued documents during his absence. In September 1108 Bohemond grants the Abbey of St. Stephen near Monopoli two vineyards near Fraxinito, and the freedom of all his lands, "*id est terra Bari Ioe Fraxiniti et Lamake et per omnes pertinentias earum et per totam terram nostram Tarenti et Orie et per omnes pertinentias illarum omni tempore quotiescumque voluerint.*"[90]

In 1108, Bohemond confirmed the possessions of the Monastery of St. Nicholas of Bari; there is some question, however, of the authenticity of the document, which purports to be a confirmation dating from March, 1230.[91] A document issued in 1109 by the *catapan*,

83. According to William of Tyre, Bohemond II was about eighteen when he went to Syria in 1127. WT, p. 589. This would place his birth approximately in 1109.

84. Suger, p. 23; Romuald. Sal., p. 414; HF, p. 483; *Historia peregrinorum*, p. 229; Matthieu d'Edesse, p. 74. The seal of Constance, affixed to a document of 1123, bears a representation of herself, with John at her right, and Bohemond the younger at her left. Engel, pl. 2, 3. If Kamal ad-Din, 3, p. 622, is correct in his reference to the capture of a son of Bohemond by Il Gazi in 1119, the captive must have been a natural son, concerning whose existence all the other sources are silent.

85. *Chartularium del monastero di s. Benedetto di Conversano*, pp. 140-142.

86. *Cod. dip. Bar.*, 5, pp. 87-88.

87. *Regii Neapolitani archivii monumenta edita ac illustrata* (Naples, 1845-1861), 5, p.314.

88. *Cod. dip. Bar.*, 5, pp. 93-94.

89. *Ibid.*, pp. 94-95.

90. *Ibid.*, 2, pp. 221-222.

91. *Ibid.*, 6, pp. 80-81.

Geoffrey of Gallipoli, shows that Bohemond is absent from Bari, for Constance is acting in his stead. [92] A number of other grants, made by Bohemond at various times, cannot be dated. In 1115, Constance confirmed the grant to the Abbey of St. Mary of Nardo of Johannes Sclavi, a fisherman of Gallipoli, together with his sons and possessions, which had been made by her husband, Bohemond. [93]

In 1133, King Roger confirmed all the privileges which Bohemond had granted to the Monastery of St. Mary of Brindisi. [94] William I confirmed the grant of a vineyard "*in territorio Sancti Petri imperialis*," which had been made to the Monastery of St. Mary in the Valley of Jehosaphat by Bohemond and Constance. [95] Bohemond is also said to have made donations to the hospice erected by Archbishop Elias of Bari for the accommodation of pilgrims coming to visit the shrine of St. Nicholas. [96]

While collecting a new army with which to return to the East, possibly with the intention of again attacking Alexius, Bohemond was taken ill and died in Apulia on March 7, 1111. [97] The dead hero was buried in the chapel adjoining the Cathedral of St. Sabinus at Canosa. The grave-chapel, unique from an architectural standpoint, is the result of a mingling of Byzantine and Saracen motives; it is almost purely Oriental, and as Bertaux has remarked, it reminds one more of a Mohammedan *turbeh* than of a Christian tomb. Above the tympanum is

---

92. *Ibid.*, 5, pp. 97-98.

93. Giovanni Guerrieri, *I conti Normanni di Nardo e di Brindisi* (1092-1130), *in Archivio storico per le province Napoletane*, 1901, 26, pp. 309-311.

94. Ughelli, 9, p. 32.

95. Garufi, p. 70.

96. Giulio Petroni, *Delia storia di Bari dagli antichi tempi sino all'anno*, 1856 (Naples, 1858-1862), 1, p. 224.

97. WT, p. 462. The exact date is given by the *Necrologium Casinense*, Muratori, 5, col. 75. It can also be determined in the following manner: Duke Roger died on February 22; *Annales Beneventani*, MGSS, 3, p. 184. According to Romualdus Salernitanus, p. 415, Bohemond died fourteen days after him, which gives us March 7. *An. Bar. Chron.*, p. 155, gives March, 1111, as the date. The following sources indicate 1111, as the year of Bohemond's death: *Chronicon s. Maxentii Pictavensis*, p. 424; *Chronicon Kemperlegiense*, p. 562; Alb., p. 686; Ord., 4, p. 243; *Chron. man. Cas.*, p. 781; *Chronicon Fossae Novae*, Muratori, 7, col. 867; Falco Beneventanus, *Chronicon*, Muratori, 5, p. 582; *Annales Cavenses*, MGSS, 3, p. 190. The two latter sources begin the year at March 1, and since they place Bohemond's death in February, they date it 1110. Anna, 2, p. 248, thinks Bohemond died not later than half a year after he returned from Durazzo. WT, 2, p. 462, places the death in the summer of 1109. The usual suspicions of poisons are not wanting. Guib., p. 254, var. 7.

the inscription:

Magnanimus siriae iacet hoc sub tegmine princeps,
Quo nullus melior nascetur in orbe deinceps,
Grecia victa quater, pars maxima partia mundi
Ingenium et vires sensere diu buamundi.
Hie acie in dena vicit virtutis arena
Agmina millena, quod et urbs sapit anthiocena.

The great bronze doors of the tomb, done in the Byzantine style, and finished in beautiful *niello* work, bear the following verses:

Unde Boatmundus, quanti fuerit Boamundus,
Graecia testatur, Syria dinumerat.
Hanc expugnavit, illam protexit ab hoste;
hinc rident Graeci, Syria, damna tua.
Quod Graecus ridet, quod Syrus luget, uterque
iuste, vera tibi sit, Boamundi, salus.

Vicit opes regum Boamundus opusque potentum
et meruit dici nomine iure suo:
intonuit terris. Cui cum succumberet orbis,
non hominem possum dicere, nolo deum.

Qui vivens studuit, ut pro Christo moreretur,
promeruit, quod ei morienti vita daretur.
Hoc ergo Christi elementia conferat isti,
militet ut coelis suus hie athleta fidelis.

Intrans cerne fores; videos, quid scribitur; ores,
ut coelo detur Boamundus ibique locetur.[98]

---

98. Schulz, 1, pp. 59-62; Bertaux, pp. 312-316; Adolf o Venturi, *Storia dell'arte italiana* (Milan, 1901-1915), 2, pp. 552, 556-560; 3, p. 409. For illustrations of the tomb, see Schulz, Atlas, Tafel 5, 2, Tafel 10, Tafel 41, 1; Bertaux, p. 313; Venturi, 2, p. 552; Jean Louis Alphonse Huillard-Bréholles, *Recherches sur les monuments et l'histoire des Normands et de la maison de Souabe dans l'Italie méridionale* (Paris, 1884), pl. 4.

Conclusion

Bohemond I, prince of Antioch, whom his son proudly styles "*Bo-amundus magnus*" in his documents, was undoubtedly one of the great men of his age. If he was less successful than either William the Conqueror or Robert Guiscard, the other two great Norman conquerors of the Middle Ages, he played for higher stakes than the former, and with slighter means at his disposal than the latter. His plans after 1104 included, I think, nothing less than the formation of a powerful Asio-European empire. [1] He already possessed in the principality of Antioch and in Apulia the eastern and western extremities of his projected empire; the conquest of his most dangerous neighbor, the Byzantine Empire, would unite the extremities and make him the greatest figure in the Mediterranean world. With the resources of the Greek Empire at his disposal, there was seemingly no limit to the possibilities of conquest: beyond Antioch lay Aleppo, and beyond Aleppo lay Bagdad. Whether or not he fully realized what might be the results of the conquest of the Empire, when he laid his plans in 1104, it is impossible to say, but it is very probable, for he was a man of clear vision and exceptional foresight.

To overthrow Alexius, however, required a greater army than he could hope to raise through his own efforts; he therefore turned to the pope for aid, and concealed behind the pontiff's plans for a Crusade his own selfish designs for personal aggrandizement. That he had attempted to exploit a religious movement for his own advantage was fully recognized by the men of his own century, [2] and this fact, coupled with the utter failure of his expedition at Durazzo did much

1. It will be recalled that, according to Richard of Poitiers, Bohemond's father had plans for the foundation of a similar empire. See *supra*, p. 24.

2. Wil. Malm., 2, p. 454; Alb., p. 652; Ord., 2, p. 449. "*Caeterum justissima Dei dispositio conatus concupiscentium invadere rent proximi sui frustrata est; inde superba conglomeratio ambitiosorum nihil eorum, quae incassum rata fiterat, adepta est.*"

to shape men's opinion of him. There can be no doubt that he, more than any other man of his time, cast discredit upon the crusading idea in Europe, and it is significant that after the Crusade of 1107, there is no great expedition to the Holy Land, until the West is aroused by the preaching of Bernard of Clairvaux, after the fall of Edessa in 1144.

I have found no reasons why the usual verdict of Bohemond's character which has ba^n handed down should be altered in any important respept; Anna Comnena, who, if she paints too favorable a pictup of her father, treats Bohemond, on the whole, very fairty, says that there were two classes of Franks who went on the Crusade: the simple folk who wished to visit the Holy Sepulchre, and the others, including Bohemond, who were bent first and foremost on conquest.[3] The princess is undoubtedly correct; Bohemond was always the *politique* and the conqueror. A typical Norman, he was brave, avaricious, wily and unscrupulous, with more than a touch of the demagogue in his composition. His undeniably great military talents were somewhat vitiated by his rashness and hotheadedness, which cost him more than one battle; he had all of the Norman's genius for statecraft, witness the stability of his Oriental principality.

A cool scepticism made him and his Norman brothers-in-arms on the First Crusade treat the pseudo-Holy Lance with scorn. He seems to have had something of his father's love for jokes and puns, [4] and, indeed, this is not the only respect in which he was like his father. Anna Comnena, who noted the resemblance between the two, said it was as if his father were the signet and he were the seal which the signet had stamped out; he was the living image of Guiscard's genius.[5] Bohemond captured Antioch in exactly the same way that Guiscard captured Durazzo in 1081; and the fact that Bohemond used an impostor to impersonate the pretender to the Greek throne, that he burned his ships at Durazzo to inspire his troops to fight with the greater desperation, and that his campaign against the Empire in 1107 follows the same lines as Guiscard's in 1081, shows a certain conscious effort on Bohemond's part to follow in his father's footsteps.

Anna Comnena, who saw the Norman in Constantinople, and

---

3. Anna, 2, p. 32.

4. Anna, 1, p. 252. The pun in William of Malmesbury, which Stubbs in a gloss has ascribed to Bohemond, is, as the text shows, to be attributed to Guiscard. Wil. Malm., 2, p. 453.

5. Anna, 1, p. 14. Cf. Benedictus de Accoltis, *Historia Gotefridi, Rec., Hist, occ.*, 5, p. 549. "*Is, militaribus artibus, magnitudine animi atque ingenis patri persimilis. . . .*"

whose husband met him at Durazzo in 1108, has given a remarkable description of his personal appearance, which deserves to be quoted in full:

> He was such a man, to speak briefly, as no one in the Empire had seen at that time, either barbarian or Greek, for he was a wonderful spectacle for the eyes, and his fame surpassed that of all others. But to describe the figure of the barbarian in detail: he was so tall, that he surpassed the tallest man by almost a cubit; he was slender of waist and flank, [6] broad of shoulder, and full-chested; his whole body was muscular, and neither thin nor fat, but very well proportioned, and shaped, so to speak, according to the canon of Polyclitus. His hands were active, and his step was firm. His head was well joined to his body, but if one looked at him rather closely, one noticed that he seemed to stoop, not as though the vertebrae or spinal column were injured, but, as it seemed, because from childhood on he had been in the habit of leaning forward somewhat.
>
> His body as a whole was very white; his face was of a mingled white and ruddy color. His hair was a shade of yellow, and did not fall upon his shoulders like that of other barbarians; the man avoided this foolish practice, and his hair was cut even to his ears. I cannot say whether his beard was red or some other color; his face had been closely shaved and seemed as smooth as gypsum; the beard, however, seems to have been red. His eyes were bluish-gray, and gave evidence of wrath and dignity; his nose and nostrils gave vent to his free breathing; his nose aided his chest, and his broad chest his nostrils, for nature has given to the air bursting forth from the heart an exit through the nostrils.
>
> The whole appearance of the man seemed to radiate a certain sweetness, but that was now cloaked by the terrors on all sides of him. There seemed to be something untamed and inexorable about his whole appearance, it seems to me, if you regarded either his size, or his countenance, and his laugh was like the roaring of other men. He was such a man in mind and body that wrath and love seemed to be bearing arms in him and waging war with each other. His mind was many-sided, versatile, and provident. His conversations were carefully worded,

---

6. Romuald. Sal., p. 415, likewise refers to his slender figure.

and his answers guarded. Being such a man, he was inferior to the emperor alone in fortune, in eloquence, and in the other natural gifts.[7]

A man of boundless ambition and inexhaustible energy, he was, in the words of Romuald of Salerno, "always seeking the impossible." [8] If he failed, however, to conquer the Byzantine Empire and establish his own great Eastern Empire, he did succeed in founding the most enduring of all the states in the Latin East.

7. Anna, 2, pp. 224–226. For character-sketches of Bohemond, see Anna, 2, p. 64; Wil. Malm., 2, pp. 454–455; Romuald. Sal., p. 415.
8. Romuald. Sal., p. 415.